D1161191

# Urban Government for Zagreb, Yugoslavia

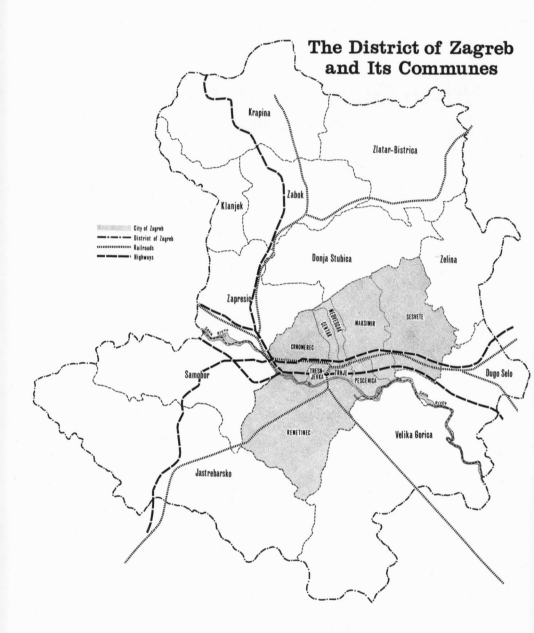

# The District of Zagreb and Its Communes

Krapina

Zlatar-Bistrica

Klanjek

Zabok

City of Zagreb
District of Zagreb
Railroads
Highways

Donja Stubica

Zelina

Zapresic

SAVA RIVER

MEDVESCAK

CENTAR

MAKSIMIR

SESVETE

CRNOMEREC

TRESN JEVKA

TRNJE

PESCENICA

Samobor

Dugo Selo

SAVA RIVER

REMETINEC

Velika Gorica

Jastrebarsko

PRAEGER SPECIAL STUDIES IN
INTERNATIONAL POLITICS AND PUBLIC AFFAIRS

# Urban Government for Zagreb, Yugoslavia

## Eugen Pusić
## Annmarie Hauck Walsh

Published in cooperation with the
Institute of Public Administration, New York

FREDERICK A. PRAEGER, Publishers
New York · Washington · London

The purpose of the Praeger Special Studies is to make specialized re-search monographs in U.S. and international economics and politics available to the academic, business, and government communities. For further information, write to the Special Projects Division, Frederick A. Praeger, Publishers, 111 Fourth Avenue, New York, N.Y. 10003.

This book is No. 3 in the series *The International Urban Studies of the Institute of Public Administration, New York*

FREDERICK A. PRAEGER, PUBLISHERS
111 Fourth Avenue, New York, N.Y. 10003, U.S.A.
77-79 Charlotte Street, London W.1, England

Published in the United States of America in 1968
by Frederick A. Praeger, Inc., Publishers

Library of Congress Catalog Card Number: 67-29437

Printed in the United States of America

# FOREWORD

This study of Zagreb is one of a series of profiles of
urban government around the world designed to provide not
only information on individual cities but also, taken together,
the raw material for comparative and general analysis of
metropolitan administration. Zagreb is examined in this
book along lines set forth in a comprehensive research out-
line applied to each of the urban areas covered in the International Urban Studies Project of the Institute of Public Administration, New York.

The international project was carried out by IPA in collaboration with the United Nations, Division of Public Administration, and with financial support from the Ford Foundation.
The results of the thirteen case studies are summarized in a
comparative volume (to be published by Frederick A. Praeger,
Inc., in 1968).

Professor Eugen Pusić conducted the research for this
book in Zagreb during 1965-66. In that effort, he received
the cooperation and help of the officers and workers of the city
administration of Zagreb. Particular thanks are due to Pero
Pirker, then president of the city assembly; to Ratko Karlović,
then secretary of the city assembly; and especially to Dr.
Stanko Brčić, assistant secretary of the city assembly, without whose sympathetic cooperation and informed advice this
study would not have been possible.

Annmarie Hauck Walsh, director of the International Urban Studies Project at IPA, collaborated with Professor Pusić
in writing this manuscript.

v

Finally, the authors wish to acknowledge the assistance and advice of many persons who have participated in the project at IPA and the United Nations, Division for Public Administration.

Lyle C. Fitch, President
Institute of Public Administration
New York

# CONTENTS

| | Page |
|---|---|
| FOREWORD | v |
| LIST OF TABLES, CHARTS, AND MAP | x |
| GLOSSARY | xi |

Chapter

| | | |
|---|---|---|
| 1 | DIMENSIONS OF THE REGION | 1 |
| | The National Context | 1 |
| | Territorial Decentralization | 2 |
| | Functional Decentralization | 4 |
| | Citizen Participation | 5 |
| | The Zagreb Urban Area | 6 |
| | The Population | 8 |
| | The Economy and Land | 11 |
| | Political Organizations | 15 |
| | Notes to Chapter 1 | 23 |
| 2 | INSTITUTIONS OF GOVERNMENT | 26 |
| | Higher-Government Organization | 27 |
| | Local Government in Zagreb | 31 |
| | The Urban Communes | 32 |
| | The City | 35 |
| | Metropolitan Powers | 40 |
| | Special Authorities | 41 |
| | Notes to Chapter 2 | 43 |
| 3 | INTERGOVERNMENTAL RELATIONSHIPS | 45 |
| | Allocation of Powers | 46 |
| | Responsibility for Urban Services | 46 |

Chapter                                              Page

        The Roles of Government Levels               48
        Financial Resources                          50
    Intergovernmental Controls                       56
        Personnel                                    56
        Legal Supervision                            58
        Fiscal Control                               59
    Behavior of the Intergovernmental System         60
    Notes to Chapter 3                               62

4   PLANNING AND PLAN IMPLEMENTATION                 64

    The National Planning System                     65
    Planning for Zagreb                              67
        Economic and Social Planning                 67
        Urban Planning in Zagreb                     70
    Implementation of Planning Choices               75
        Economic Plans                               75
        Urban Plan                                   78
    Evaluation of Planning in the Zagreb Area        82
    Notes to Chapter 4                               85

5   SELECTED URBAN SERVICES                          86

    Water Supply                                     86
        Water Finance                                91
        Organizational Issues                        92
        Appraisal                                    94
        Planning for Water-Supply Expansion          94
    Public Housing                                   99
        The Housing Agencies                         103
        Finance of Public Housing                    105
        Planning and Rates of Investment             106
        Problems of Housing Construction             109
    Mass Passenger Transportation                    110
        The Zagreb Electrical Tramway
            Corporation                              113
        Transportation Problems                      115
        Transportation Planning                      118
        Investment in Transportation Expansion       120
        Interagency Relationships                    121

Chapter                                                      Page

        Primary and Secondary Education              123
            Social Management                             126
            Government Education Agencies               126
            Educational Finance                         129
        Notes to Chapter 5                              131

6    ISSUES OF URBAN GOVERNMENT                 134

        Notes to Chapter 6                              149

POSTSCRIPT                                               150

ABOUT THE AUTHORS                                  151

## LIST OF TABLES, CHARTS, AND MAP

### TABLES

Page

1   Subdivisions of Zagreb:  Area and Population   7

2   Demographic Characteristics (1961 Census)   10

3   General-Government Expenditures in
      Yugoslavia   51

4   Local-Government Expenditures in the Zagreb
      Urban Area   52

5   General-Government Revenue Sources   54

6   Projected Shifts in Land Use in Seven Urban
      Communes of Zagreb   74

7   Authorized Expenditure on Mala Mlaka
      Water-Supply Project   98

8   Total Rolling Stock, Zagreb   116

### CHARTS

1   City Assembly of Zagreb (1964)   36

2   Zagreb City Administration (1964)   38

3   The Water System Corporation of Zagreb (1964)   87

4   The Department of Building, Communal, and
      Housing Affairs of the City of Zagreb (1964)   90

### MAP

1   The District of Zagreb and Its Communes   ii

# GLOSSARY

Assemblies
Elected representative organs of government at each level--federal, republic, district, and commune.

Chambers
The separate houses of the bicameral or multicameral assemblies. Also, the economic chambers, which are autonomous associations of enterprises within various industries.

Communes
The basic units of local government in Yugoslavia, comparable to municipalities. The entire territory of the nation is subdivided into communes of similar structure.

Councils
The executive boards selected by communal or city assemblies. They include both assembly members and laymen; they prepare draft decisions for the local assemblies; and they supervise local administration on behalf of the assemblies.

Functional
decentralization
The concept in Yugoslav political theory of delegating management powers for economic, social, and public-service functions to separate specialized institutions, such as single-purpose public corporations and institutions.

Republics
The six states of the Yugoslav Federation. Croatia is the republic of which Zagreb is the capital.

Working organizations
All independent operating institutions, including productive enterprises, public-service corporations, and

other special authorities, managed by workers' councils that are representative of the organization's employees.

Zagreb "central-city" area

An area designated for purposes of planning and land control, approximating seven of the nine communes of Zagreb City.

Zagreb City

The urban portion of Zagreb District, including nine urban communes. Over this jurisdiction, the Zagreb District government exercises powers of city government. This jurisdiction is also referred to as the "urban" or "metropolitan" area.

Zagreb District

The larger jurisdiction of Zagreb government, including twenty communes in total. This area encompasses the city as well as a vast rural hinterland.

# Urban Government for Zagreb, Yugoslavia

CHAPTER **1** DIMENSIONS OF THE
REGION

## THE NATIONAL CONTEXT

Pursuing themes of political unity and administrative
pluralism, Yugoslavia is making innovations in government and
political organization as well as economic management. The
organization of public administration, particularly arrangements for local government, has been evolving for the past
fifteen years; the country intends to continue an explicit effort to adjust government structures to the social and political
values expressed by the nation's ideology and constitution.
In most areas of the world, local governments have a high degree of structural stability, but in Yugoslavia they have been
changing faster than the urban environment; local powers and
institutions present a moving target for description.

Since 1950, the principles underlying adjustments in
organization have sought to maximize administrative decentralization and citizen participation within the limits of efficient administration, economic development, and political
unity. The over-all aim of these adjustments is to deconcentrate power, to fragment--by both territory and function--
administrative authority throughout society. From the end of
World War II to 1950, government in Yugoslavia was a tightly
organized hierarchy within which local governments and
economic enterprises were essentially administrative arms
of central authorities. The largest body of decisions affecting
urban economic and physical development was embodied in
central plans and applied by central bureaucracies. Party
organizations were closely involved in government direction.
At present, the system is described as "evolving commu-
nalism"; the continuing trends have been toward greater autonomy and powers for both territorially and functionally decentralized units at the level of the commune, and toward a
shift in decision-making from government and Party bureaucracies to elected officials and citizen groups. These three

1

principles--territorial decentralization, functional decentralization, and citizen participation--underlie a constellation
of political, governmental, and economic developments in
Yugoslavia.

### Territorial Decentralization

Yugoslavia emerged from World War II with numerous
small "local people's committees of liberation" formed during
the war to replace the traditional local structures, which had
been taken over by the occupying enemy forces. These committees, considered too small for local government, were
gradually enlarged and reduced in number, and in 1952 they
were renamed "communes," the traditional term for local
governments. [1]

In 1952, the roles and duties of local-government bodies
and those of the local committees of the political Party were
distinguished and separated. [2] Locally elected committees of
the communes were established as basic units of local administration. The federal Constitutional Law of 1953 conferred
upon these units considerable powers previously assigned to republic and federal authorities.

In the meantime, a series of adjustments was made in
territorial jurisdictions below the level of the six republics
that comprise the Yugoslav federation. These modifications
are illustrated in the following list of local units in the nation:

| Year | Regions | Districts | Cities | Communes | Local People's Committees |
|------|---------|-----------|--------|----------|---------------------------|
| 1946 | 2  | 407 | 81  | -     | 11,556 |
| 1949 | 23 | 344 | 198 | -     | 7,782  |
| 1952 | -  | 327 | 265 | 3,811 | -      |
| 1955 | -  | 107 | 2   | 1,479 | -      |
| 1960 | -  | 75  | 2   | 774   | -      |
| 1964 | -  | 40  | 2   | 577   | -      |

After 1955, the growth in size of the communes and concomitant reduction in number were dictated by the large share of
powers conferred upon them and by their need for a broad
economic base sufficient for meaningful autonomy. In 1963,
the average Yugoslav commune had 33,000 inhabitants and

covered 170 square miles.  This is unusually large by international comparison.  Smaller bodies were established within
the communes in order to maintain citizen participation and
a more personal contact with administration.  In 1960, there
were some 12, 000 neighborhood associations, or "political
outposts of the communes, " and 3, 300 local agencies, or
"administrative outposts of the communes, " both organized
in the villages or urban neighborhoods that compose the communes.

In recent years, the second-tier local-government units--
districts--have also grown proportionately larger in size and
smaller in number, assuming a regional character. [3]  Since
1963, districts have existed at the discretion of the six republic governments.  By 1966, there were twenty-eight, found
only in two republics--Serbia and Croatia.  They are flexible
units, whose responsibilities differ according to size, density
and internal characteristics.  Commonly, districts are used
for coordination and technical assistance to communes, and
their powers are generally delegated to them by republics
and communes.  They have also proved useful mechanisms
for adaptation to metropolitan growth.  Districts are an average 2, 500 square miles, with 475, 000 people.

The formal structure of local authorities is uniform
throughout Yugoslavia, with the exception of two districts,
Zagreb and Belgrade, which have the title of cities, partly in
deference to tradition and to the dominance of urban complexes
in these districts.  In other large cities in Yugoslavia, separate urban communes that geographically constitute a single
city are empowered to establish a federation, with common
institutions and with powers transferred from the communes.

The Yugoslav Constitution of April 7, 1963, represented
a major step toward decentralization, with its general allocation of powers to the communes.  These are now basic units
of administration on which the central government depends
for implementing most public-service programs.  National
political theory posits continued shrinking of the national
bureaucracy, with concomitant growth in the functions of local
units.

## Functional Decentralization

A system of functional self-government is developing in Yugoslavia, based on autonomy and self-management of economic and public-service institutions. Workers' self-management--management of institutions by elected councils of employees--was introduced in economic enterprises in 1950. From 1952 to 1962, this principle was applied to the management of agencies and institutions for public utilities, education, health, welfare, social security, culture, research, and housing. The Yugoslav Constitution of 1963 accepts functional self-government as fundamental to the structure of society generally and introduces the concept of a working organization, which encompasses economic and public-service institutions in any field. The working organization--albeit a school, a hospital, or a productive enterprise--is in principle independent from general government and is managed by elected representatives of the people working in it. Thus, while urban land and the major means of production are generally publicly owned in Yugoslavia, they are not owned and managed by government. The distinction is a meaningful one; operating institutions manage their assets in trust for the public and are formally supervised by government only for the legality of their actions.

The aim of functional decentralization, like that of territorial decentralization, is for the entire state structure to eventually place day-to-day decision-making powers over social matters in the hands of particular representative bodies at the lowest level, in both public administration and economic enterprise. This transformation is under way and in theory will develop to the point at which each enterprise and public service will operate as an independent entity in an open-market environment; general governments will function merely as clearinghouses for exchanging information and for cooperative planning on a territorial basis. Speculation at present contemplates ultimately a system in which associations of self-managed enterprises and agencies will coordinate the activities of their members, perform services of common interest for all agencies of a single type, and provide a forum in which their representatives can adjust conflicts of interest. Eventually such functionally organized associations at each territorial level might even replace general local and regional governments altogether.

## Citizen Participation

The third major principle of the decentralization process is maximizing citizen participation in organization and decision-making of both government and enterprise. Steps to implement this principle have included the institution of workers' council management, representative local-government assemblies with rotating membership, social-management boards in such fields as education and housing, voters' meetings, and neighborhood associations. Moreover, in order to strengthen the citizen's role, several moves have been made to increase the power of elected assemblies vis-à-vis administrative and Party bureaucracies.

All these mechanisms, as they appear in Zagreb, will be described in detail later in this book. Now it is important to keep in mind that they have been designed with a precise theoretical purpose in view--to create a system of socialist democracy in which every individual participates directly in both the political and the economic decision-making that affects his life, and in which the impact of a central bureaucracy is minimized and perhaps even eliminated. The aim is to involve as many people as possible, in one way or another, in debate and decision-making. The patterns of functional and territorial decentralization, together with strengthening and augmenting citizen participation, are considered means for attaining such a system. While problems and setbacks have been encountered in all three areas of development, the modifications represent attempts to guide a changing system toward the perceived goal of a society of autonomous, self-regulated organizations, interrelated and coordinated through free relationships and mutual associations. Because of these attempts, trends in Yugoslav urban government contrast with those in most other countries, where the role of government generally, and the central government particularly, is growing.

Underlying administrative pluralism in the Yugoslav system, and to some degree making it feasible, is unity of fundamental policy. The basic orientation for the development of government organization is founded in ideology and fundamental policies worked out at the national level. These provide the tactical and strategic goals that guide the thinking of leadership at all levels. Thus, although the central government and political organizations have divested themselves of

direct control and management in many matters, they remain
social regulators protecting and promoting the fundamental
values of Yugoslavia's philosophy and Constitution. In the
Yugoslav view, decentralized social management is an alternative form of democracy to a competitive political system.

The organization of government for Zagreb illustrates
some of the unique aspects of administration that are elements
of this evolving system. And the major issues and problems
of urban government in Zagreb are outgrowths of the general
attempt to create the most decentralized system of administration consonant with achieving economic and social goals.
These are issues of developing the competency of small units
of government, organizing public-service enterprises on a
scale large enough to provide complex urban services efficiently without sacrificing local autonomy and public participation, and striking a balance between coordination of policy
and fragmentation of authority within the urban area.

## THE ZAGREB URBAN AREA

Zagreb is the second largest urban complex in Yugoslavia (after Belgrade) and the capital of Croatia, one of the
six republics of the Federation of Yugoslavia. The Assembly
of Croatia defined the various local authority jurisdictions in
and around Zagreb. These include the District of Zagreb, and
within it twenty communes, of which nine in the center form
the urban area, or "city," of Zagreb. (See map on frontispiece.)

Delineation of these jurisdictions was based on several
policies: that the units of local government and administration
in the urban area be small enough for effective citizen participation and organized in such a way that the opinion of the
local population carry weight; that administrative services be
within easy reach of the users; that territory necessary for
future urban development be encompassed by the defined urban
area; that the area represent a rational unit for economic development; and finally, that the historical boundaries of cities
and urban neighborhoods be respected wherever possible.

The District of Zagreb includes, in addition to the urban
area, a wide expanse of rural land. Some 822,000 people

live within its 1,550 square miles and twenty communes. Within it, the Zagreb urban area, defined as the jurisdiction for city government, embraces nine communes and some 480,000 persons on 250 square miles.

TABLE 1

Subdivisions of Zagreb:  Area and Population

| Jurisdiction | Square Miles | 1961 Population |
|---|---|---|
| Zagreb District | 1,550 | 821,684 |
| Urban area (City) | 250 | 479,717 |
| Centar* | 5.6 | 63,617 |
| Črnomerec* | 30.7 | 83,442 |
| Maksimir* | 41.7 | 77,942 |
| Medveščak* | 6.9 | 57,476 |
| Peščenica* | 9.8 | 26,947 |
| Trešnjevka* | 4.8 | 71,147 |
| Trnje* | 2.6 | 51,277 |
| Remetinec | 89.4 | 27,492 |
| Sesvete | 60.0 | 20,377 |
| Rest of district | | |
| (11 rural communes) | 1,300 | 340,600 |

* Included in "central-city" portion.

Seven of these nine communes form the traditional "central city" area of some 100 square miles. [4] The rest of the urban area consists of land designated for future urban development. However, even the central-city area includes a great deal of land that is not built up: More than 50 per cent of this territory is used for agricultural and other rural purposes, and some 25 per cent is covered by parks of the northern recreational zone.

Manifold village settlements are located within the Zagreb urban area. For example, there are 87 in Remetinec and Sesvete, the two urban-area communes that are not considered part of the central-city portion. The difference in size and density of the central communes and the outer ones is striking. Remetinec and Sesvete cover 89 and 60 square miles, respectively, and have population densities per square mile, as of 1961, of 308 and 340; in contrast, two of the central industrialized communes (Trešnjevka and Trnje) are 4.8 and 2.6 square miles and had 1961 densities of 15,000 and 20,000, respectively. [5] Communal boundaries in low-density areas have been drawn in such a way as to encompass sizable populations. Thus, although that part of the urban area of Zagreb that lies outside the dense central-city area consists structurally of some 87 villages, it is organized as two communes with populations of more than 20,000 each.

While the residential population of the Zagreb urban area is thus highly concentrated in the center (more than 90 per cent is in the central city portion), people commute to work and to sell their agricultural produce from the outer portions of the urban area as well as from rural communes in the Zagreb District. The main territory from which people commute is immediately north of the city, where comparatively poor agricultural land is located. Relatively few people commute, however; about 10 per cent of those employed in Zagreb in 1957 lived outside it. [6]

## The Population

The growth of Zagreb, like that of other urban areas in Yugoslavia, is far outstripping the growth of the nation as a whole, as steady urbanization of a traditionally peasant society progresses. In 1960, half the nation's population derived its major income from agriculture, as compared with 75 per cent

in 1938.  By 1961, about one quarter of the Yugoslav population resided in the 176 urban places with a population of more
than 5,000; most of these lived in towns of less than 100,000.

The population of the Zagreb urban area increased 22
per cent between 1953 and 1961, while the population of the
nation increased about 9 per cent and that of the Republic of
Croatia about 6 per cent.  (The increase for the District of
Zagreb was about 10 per cent. )  The over-all rate of population growth between 1953 and 1961 was the same for the urban
area and for the central-city portion of it.  However, several
communes experienced extremely rapid growth, particularly
Peščenica, with an average annual increase of almost 11 per
cent.  The rural parts of the Zagreb District lost population
to the urban area.  The population of the eleven rural communes declined about 2. 5 per cent.

More than 85 per cent of the growth of the Zagreb urban
area from 1953 to 1961 was due to migration.  The rising tide
of rural to urban migration has tended to overtake industrial
development and the increase in employment opportunities, and
to overtax housing and public facilities.  Existing problems
in coping with growth are underscored by the projections by
city planning authorities of a population of nearly 1 million--
double the present size--by the year 2000.

The Zagreb urban area differs significantly from the
nation in several demographic characteristics in a pattern
typical of urban centers in predominantly rural nations.  (See
Table 2. )  The population of the urban area bulges in the
working-age bracket.  The Zagreb urban area has a very high
literacy rate of 96 per cent compared with approximately 80
per cent for the nation as a whole; its death rate is somewhat
lower and its birth rate is considerably lower than the national
average.  A total of 70 per cent of the households in the urban
area have three or fewer members, in contrast to 46 per
cent in Yugoslavia.

The people of Zagreb are relatively homogeneous in a
heterogeneous nation.  Yugoslavia was formed after World
War I from areas that had historically been divided under
Austrian and Turkish control and on which several peoples
of common Slav stock resided.  About 40 per cent of the national population is Serb, and some 25 per cent is Croatian;

other major population groups are the Slovenes, Macedonians, and Montenegrins. Zagreb is the traditional center and capital of Croatia, and almost 90 per cent of its population is Croatian. Most of the immigration into the urban area originates within the Croatian Republic:

## TABLE 2

### Demographic Characteristics
(1961 Census)

|  | Yugoslavia | Zagreb Urban Area |
|---|---|---|
| Percentage of population growth, 1953-61 | 9 | 22 |
| Females per 100 males | 105 | 113 |
| Percentage of population aged 0-14 | 31 | 20 |
| Percentage of population aged 15-44 | 44 | 50 |
| Percentage of population aged 45-59 | 15 | 19 |
| Percentage of population over 60 | 10 | 12 |
| Percentage of those over ten who are illiterate | 20 | 4 |
| Death rate | 9.0 | 7.8 |
| Birth rate | 22.7 | 13.3 |
| Percentage of households of 3 or fewer members | 46 | 70 |

## The Economy and Land

The City of Zagreb, situated between the mountain Medvednica in the north and the Sava River to the south, has a favorable location on international communications routes. It benefits from several natural assets--including a moderate climate and graded topography of moderate altitude, with wooded mountains, foothills, and plains with abundant water-- that allow for both efficient growth and substantial recreational facilities within the city boundaries.

Zagreb was founded in the eleventh century as a religious-feudal community adjoining the fortified town of Gradec in the highlands north of the present city center. The two communities grew slowly and steadily for centuries, until they were united in the nineteenth century. Lying at the crossroads of major trade routes and in a favorable economic and geographic position, Zagreb became an important commercial center, particularly for the exchange of goods between West and East. The development of industry and building of the railroad at the end of the nineteenth century triggered rapid growth and intense land speculation, producing largely uncontrolled and unplanned expansion between the foothills and the Sava River and out to the east and west on a linear pattern. This ballooning "lower city," with its growing industrial district, was given further impetus after World War I, when the Yugoslav nation was created and industrialization was accelerated to supply goods previously produced in Austria and Hungary.[7]

The major industrial sectors are just south of the railroad, which bisects the center of town, gradually extending farther south to the river. The heaviest residential concentration remains in the old section of the city near the foothills in the north, where density in single-family residences has remained stable. Unlike cities in the United States, the core of Zagreb has maintained its character; newer migrants have settled in the sectors of new apartment houses and single-family dwellings--some of low quality--east and west of the city center and scattered in the industrial zone. There are major administrative institutions and upper-income residential sections in the northern hills, where the medieval origins of the city lay. Farther north, the mountains and woodlands provide a major recreational area for the urban population.

Commercial and trade activities have been highly concentrated in the center of the city, just north of the railroad.
Thus, both commercial and industrial employment is concentrated in the center of the urban area, while residential development has expanded broadly to the east and west and
gradually toward the river on the south.  These patterns of
development were largely responses to geographic factors--
the barrier of the hills in the north and the river to the south--
and to east-west transportation axes.

At present, Zagreb is the highway and railway hub of
northern Yugoslavia, situated on the major north-south rail
axis and the western route to Yugoslavia's most important
port, Rijeka, on the Adriatic Sea.  The city of Zagreb con-
tains more industrial enterprises--employing some 53,000 per-
sons--than any other Yugoslav city.  Although the Yugoslav
Government and planners have made efforts in recent years to
decentralize industrial location, in 1958 some 44 per cent of
all industrial enterprises were located in seven cities, led by
Zagreb.  With slightly more than 2 per cent of the nation's
population, the Zagreb urban area accounts for 5.7 per cent
of its nonagricultural employment, 6.9 per cent of its gross
national product, 7.9 per cent of total retail sales, and 11 per
cent of total value added by processing and manufacturing. [8]

In 1961, of the total work force of more than 280,000 in
the entire Zagreb District, some 223,000 were statistically
identified by economic sector of employment.  Approximately
30 per cent were employed in manufacturing, 10 per cent in
building and transport, 11 per cent in crafts, 25 per cent in
services,[9] 8 per cent in trade, and 10 per cent in mining,
agriculture, and forestry.[10]  By 1965, 92,000 out of 234,000
employees were classified as in industry and mining.

In terms of national income[11] in the urban area, however, industry is considerably more dominant than employment statistics would indicate.  In 1962, the total national income in the urban area was some 226 billion dinars, of which
industry and mining accounted for about 66 per cent.  Second
in importance were trade and commerce, which produced
approximately 18 per cent, followed by building and crafts,
each of which provided about 8 per cent.

Of employed persons in the urban area, about 40 per
cent are white collar and 60 per cent are blue collar.  Of the

former, some two thirds have secondary or higher education, and of the latter, nearly one third are skilled or highly skilled. Average per capita salaries of employed persons in the area are relatively high for the nation (480,000 dinars per year, or $384 at the official exchange rate).[12] The value of total personal income is nearly twice this figure, however, due to employer contributions for free medical services, family allowances, pensions, and other benefits and public services[13] that supplement salaries.

The number of unemployed as of June 30, 1964, in the Zagreb urban area was 11,487, which is on the order of 5 per cent of the total working population. It should be noted that almost 9,000 were women; specifically, 7,000 of the unemployed were unskilled women seeking blue-collar jobs.[14]

Most economic activities in Zagreb are in the public sector, that is, within socially owned enterprises. This sector accounted for almost 90 per cent of the national income produced in the Zagreb District in 1962. Both productive enterprises and many activities that would usually be considered public service and public administration are provided by autonomous working organizations, whose assets are publicly owned but managed by the institutions' workers' councils. The total value of capital investment in the urban area in 1962 was roughly 20 per cent of the national income produced in the area; these investments were financed by the various enterprises from their own depreciation and investment funds, from bank loans, and by the investment funds of communes, the city, the republic, and the Federation of Yugoslavia under provisions of yearly economic- and social-development plans.

Since 1950, the economic system has been progressively decentralized, first by endowing workers' management bodies with responsibility for the disposition of increasing portions of the economic values they produce and, second, by conferring upon local authorities more and more of the governmental powers of regulation in economic matters. At the same time, policies regarding private craftsmen have been liberalized under federal law. A shop may be established by any person who can prove that he has the required skill to perform the craft involved, and it may employ up to five persons without being considered an industrial enterprise that would come under the rule for workers' management as a public trust.

The objective of economic-development policy in Zagreb is, first, to stabilize economic growth, which proceeded during the last decade at a high rate but with unbalancing effects on the relationship between various branches and sectors of the economy; and second, to stimulate further growth in the branches of industry on which the Zagreb economic region has traditionally relied, particularly electrical and chemical industries. The index of industrial production for the Zagreb urban area, with 1962 representing a base of 100, was 79 in 1959, 91 in 1960, 95 in 1961, 100 in 1962, and 113 in 1963. Most large new enterprises are begun by existing economic enterprises. (Thus, 26 out of the 40 enterprises established in 1964 were initiated by existing companies.) In addition, communes, neighborhood associations, and other nongovernment organizations, as well as groups of private citizens, initiate small enterprises. Neighborhood associations have been active in creating local service establishments, such as laundries, playgrounds, and nurseries. Groups of citizens frequently organize housing cooperatives for construction of family homes for their own use, and these cooperatives are registered as economic enterprises.

The emerging economic system of public enterprises operating in a partly competitive market situation but under the general coordinating guidance of local government renders highly important the development of competent local administration and planning. The task of maintaining a balance between the autonomy of public enterprises and fulfillment of general public interest and coordinated economic development is considered a challenging one. The ultimate goal of the developing system is that regulation and coordination shall be provided not so much by government planning as by voluntary cooperation of related enterprises participating in broad associations, and that the general interests shall be protected by the citizen's dual role as participant in both the management of the economic institution in which he works and in the administration of general local government. Thus, as we shall see in the following chapter, the structure of local government intimately links economic institutions with local-government councils.

Enterprises are legally independent, and the Yugoslav plans are not directly binding upon them. A workers' council is elected by all the employees of the organization, and it undertakes day-to-day management through an executive board

elected by that council from its members or from all employees.  The councils have decision-making competency
over operations, including determination of what to produce
and how; prices (with exceptions); wages; investment and
distribution of surpluses; and personnel.  A workers' council
is elected for a two-year term, and usually has from 15 to
200 members, depending on the size of the enterprise.  As
only one third of the members of the executive board may be
re-elected for successive terms, a large number of employees
will participate over time in management of the institution.
The director or manager of an enterprise is an ex officio
member of the executive board.  Candidates for that post are
nominated by a special committee on which members of the
workers' council and the local-government assembly sit.  The
director is appointed from those so nominated by the workers'
council.

Economic associations have been established outside the
general government framework to stimulate coordination for
economic development.  These associations, or "chambers,"
to which enterprises must belong and in which they must participate, group together institutions in various industrial
categories.  They develop broad economic policies; make
recommendations on production and sales; represent their
members before government bodies and in obtaining bank
loans; and attempt to harmonize the particular interests of
various enterprises with the public interest.  Since 1958,
representatives of government bodies are members of the
economic chambers, along with representatives of the member enterprises.  This arrangement illustrates the Yugoslav
policy of shifting regulatory functions from the formal government bureaucracy to special institutions, and of having the
economic organizations themselves participate in regulating
and coordinating activities.  Major economic institutions are
highly influential in Zagreb, and their particular plans form
the basis of communal economic plans, which are in turn integrated into the city plan.


## POLITICAL ORGANIZATIONS

In light of attempts to maximize the operating autonomy
of government and economic institutions throughout the country, political organizations in Yugoslavia play particularly
important roles of coordination and policy formulation in the

system. They are intended to bind together otherwise pur-
posefully fragmented administration and management. The
predominant political institution in Yugoslavia is the League
of Communists, successor to the Communist Party of Yugoslavia, which played a major historical role in unifying and
liberating the nation. Communist Party members won municipal elections in Zagreb and Belgrade as early as 1920, soon
after the nation was created in 1918. After 1929, there was
little competitive political activity within the Kingdom of Yugoslavia and considerable conflict between the Serb and Croatian
sectors of the population. The German invasion in 1941 and
subsequent occupation brought an end to the kingdom, and the
Communist Party organized armed resistance during the war
and after the liberation of the country with the Allied victory
in Europe. The Party was, during the war and afterward, the
nucleus of a broad national-front movement seeking to include
all citizens who were in agreement with a program of national
independence and unity and of revolutionary political and social
reform. The major points of that program were equality of
the different nationalities within Yugoslavia under a federal
and republican form of government, public control over means
of production, and stimulation of economic development. The
Communist Party organized Yugoslavia on a highly centralized
pattern immediately after the war, when the tasks of economic
reconstruction were tremendous. During subsequent years,
the Party and the national front developed the policies of decentralization and broad self-government in all fields of public life and community interest.

The Communist Party changed its name in 1952 to the
League of Communists of Yugoslavia. A mass political organization, of which the League remains the center, was
created--the Socialist Alliance of Working People of Yugoslavia (the former "National Front"). These two political organizations are part of the organic legal structure of the nation,
and their purposes and roles are defined in the preamble to
the Constitution of Yugoslavia of 1963. The Constitution provides:

> Under conditions of socialist democracy and
> social self-government, the League of Com-
> munists, acting through the spreading of ideas
> and by political methods, is the prime initi-
> ator of political activity for the protection and
> furtherance of the achievements of the socialist

revolution and socialist relations in the community, and particularly for the strengthening
of the socialist and democratic social consciousness of the people. [15]

The Constitution provides further that the Socialist Alliance shall discuss and make decisions on questions from all
fields of social life, express evaluations of the operations of
government organs and working organizations, take political
initiatives, and work for the development of socialist and
democratic relationships among people.  The Alliance actively
tries to get people involved in political discussion--in local
assemblies, trade unions, and other organizations.  Its Sixth
Congress, held in 1966, underscored its responsibility to ensure that the electoral procedures and rotation of elective
offices work properly and fairly.

The role of these political institutions is primarily to
develop and to promote the fundamental values and policies of
the nation, not to govern directly; to mobilize and aggregate
opinion, not to administer.  As of 1952, local Party secretaries cannot also be heads of local-government bodies, and
are instructed not to interfere in the day-to-day affairs of
local government and administration.  On the other hand,
Party members are encouraged to participate in all local-
government and enterprise units and to influence through their
individual participation the policy of those units.  Administrative officials are encouraged to consider the political im-
plications of their decisions, and Party and elected officials
are encouraged to acquire technical and administrative competency.  Politics and administration are closely  interrelated
in that the fundamental values of the society developed and
expressed through the political organizations form the basis
for administrative activity.  One role of the League of Communists and the Socialist Alliance is to intensify this relationship by heightening the political consciousness of both citizens
and administrators, and coordinating the fundamental policy
bases of administrative activity.

Civil servants have the right to participate in all political activities, to vote, and to be elected to representative
bodies of central and local government (except that they are
not to be elected to representative bodies in the same unit of
government in which they are employed).  In practice, they
make considerable use of these rights.  In addition, the trade

union of public servants must be consulted in an advisory capacity on all draft laws and regulations concerning the civil-service system.

The membership of the League of Communists (as of 1963) is 1,019,013, or about 15 per cent of the population over eighteen years of age. The League of Communists is conceived of as the most active core of the Alliance. Its concrete aims, listed in the preamble to its rules, are: national independence, equality and unity of Yugoslav nationalities, social control of the means of production, self-government in all fields of social life, and internationalism conceived as an equal cooperation of all nations toward human progress. [16]

The League of Communists was traditionally the political organization of the working class, while the Socialist Alliance aspires to maximum membership without orientation to a specific group. Today both organizations are heterogeneous as to occupation of their members and include people of all Yugoslav nationalities. Of the total membership of the League of Communists, roughly 368,000 are workers, 88,000 are peasants, 388,000 are employees, 36,000 are students, 59,000 are members of the armed forces, and 80,000 have other occupations.

The foundation of the League organization consists of units in working enterprises and institutions as well as in urban neighborhoods and rural villages. These basic units annually elect a secretary or secretariat and delegates to conferences at a higher level. These conferences elect executive committees, a president, a secretary, and delegates to a still higher level, generally that of the commune. Similarly structured Party units exist at the level of the district, the republic, and finally the federation, with conferences at the lower territorial level successively electing delegates to those of the higher level. The highest organ of the League of Communists is the National Congress, convened every five years, which elects a central committee and a control commission. The central committee elects from among its members an executive committee, which has included a secretary-general and several secretaries. [17] The control commission is responsible for supervising the financial management of the League and reviewing disciplinary decisions taken by the different bodies of the League against its members.

Local units of the Socialist Alliance are organized in villages and urban neighborhoods. Each elects its own president and once every two years chooses delegates to a local conference that is held for the territory of several local units. Like the League of Communists, each unit in the Alliance elects delegates to a higher-level unit up to the level of the federation. The highest body of the Alliance is its congress, which is convened every five years and elects a national committee and a control committee. Thus, the higher bodies in both political organizations are indirectly elected by local membership. In matters of policy and operations, lower-level bodies are bound by decisions taken at higher levels, according to the procedures of "democratic centralism."[18]

Both political organizations have decisive influence on the major policies of representative assemblies at all territorial levels of government. The members of the assemblies are without exception members of the Socialist Alliance, and the preponderant majority belong to the League of Communists. League members fill 661 of the 670 seats in the Federal Assembly, 434 out of 440 seats of the Assembly of the Republic of Croatia, 222 of 240 seats in the Zagreb City Assembly, and 1,565 out of 2,029 seats in the commune assemblies within the City of Zagreb. The members of the assemblies, however, are not necessarily members of the governing bodies of the political organizations; these bodies exert their influence in an indirect and mainly informal way. They are, however, instrumental in nominating candidates for the assemblies and in organizing the mechanisms of political control over them, such as voters' meetings, referendums, and recalls. They are often involved informally in candidacies for individual posts and offices, from directorships of economic enterprises to presidencies of representative assemblies. The individual office-holders in central and local government as well as officers of the largest nongovernment organizations, such as trade unions, are more often than not members of the committees of the political organizations.

Under republic law, citizens are supposed to participate directly, as well as through the Socialist Alliance, in putting up candidates for elective office. The principal method of direct participation is through the voters' meeting, which is organized for approximately every 500 voters and in which every citizen is entitled to submit the name of a candidate. The meeting as a whole accepts or rejects the candidacy by majority vote. In addition, any group of fifty citizens can submit a nomination in writing to the communal election commission. The election commissions must accept every candidacy that satisfies the requirements of law. In practice, however, most candidates are put up by voters' meetings.

The last general elections in the Zagreb urban area were held in June, 1962, for the communal chambers of the communal assemblies, and in June, 1963, for the chambers of working organizations of the communal assemblies. [19] In 1963, 590 candidates contested the 524 seats in the communal assemblies of the Zagreb urban area, while 731 candidates contested the 501 seats in the 11 rural communes of the Zaggreb District. The significantly larger number of uncontested elections in the urban section of the district is probably in part the result of greater interest in local politics in rural communities, where one commune consists of several villages and people are motivated by intervillage rivalries. More rigorous studies of political behavior should throw more light on other factors that may play a role in this interesting discrepancy. The local organizations of the Socialist Alliance participated actively in nominating candidates, and most of the candidates had at least passive endorsement of those organizations. Given the large number of posts and candidates, these organizations as a rule exercise no more than passive acceptance except for those candidates who are to be sent by the communal assemblies to the city assembly. The members of the latter are elected by the communal assemblies from among their own membership. (This election took place in June, 1963.)

The major elective offices in the urban area are president of the city assembly, its two vice-presidents, the chairmen of its chambers, committees, and councils; and the presidents of the communal assemblies, their vice-presidents, the chairmen of their chambers, and of their committees and councils. These officers are elected by the respective assemblies. The presidents, vice-presidents, and chairmen of the chambers are elected for four-year terms and cannot be re-elected for a second consecutive term, but they may be recalled at any time by the full assemblies or their chambers. The chairmen of committees and councils are elected for two years and their eligibility is limited to two terms. They also may be recalled.

Nongovernment organizations play an important role in the public life in Yugoslavia generally and in the large urban areas particularly. The larger organizations that pursue aims closely related to the public interest are collective members of the Socialist Alliance, and the most important ones have interlocking governing bodies with the Alliance and the League of Communists. In the Zagreb urban area, the most important nongovernment organizations are the trade unions and the economic chambers. Each trade union, organized by branch of activity (manufacturing, building, services, etc.), has committees at each territorial level--commune, district, republic, and nation--as well as units within each relevant enterprise or institution. In addition, the Association of Trade Unions of Yugoslavia has coordinating bodies at each level, culminating in a general congress of the trade unions and its central committee. The trade unions play a major educational and initiating role within the system of workers' management. They organize and influence the elections of management bodies, and the preparation of the charter and other internal regulations of enterprises. They take a major part in discussions on distribution of the institution's income, and are consulted by city and commune authorities in the preparation of various plans of economic and social development. To take a recent example of their influence, the Zagreb City Assembly for several months deferred a decision to raise fares in public transportation pursuant to the expressed opinion of trade-union representatives.

The economic chambers are major initiators of area-wide economic activities and are often the source of proposals for economic and social development plans or other economic measures taken by local governments. Their representatives take an active part in the deliberations and decisions of the economic chamber of the Zagreb City Assembly.

In addition, the workers' councils within each economic enterprise and self-governing organization are directly linked to local government, as they elect representatives to the chamber of working organizations of each communal assembly. These chambers of the communal assemblies elect the members to three out of the four chambers of the Zagreb City Assembly.

A considerable number of other nongovernment organizations are consulted by local authorities in preparing economic

and social development plans, and participate in local policy-
making by presenting public proposals and through their representatives in the various councils and committees of local
government.  These include the Association of Veterans, the
Red Cross, the Association of "Our Children, " the Chapter
of Emigrants of Croatia, societies for the advancement of
technical education, sporting and recreational associations,
and professional associations.

Finally, a very large number of citizens participate
formally in local decision-making.  Election procedures are
utilized, as noted, for selecting governing bodies both
for general government at various territorial levels and
for economic and public-service enterprises.  Zagreb citizens
participate directly in neighborhood voters' meetings, elections
to the communal assemblies, elections to the managing boards
of the housing developments in which they live, and elections
to neighborhood councils.  They sit on school boards, local-
assembly executive councils, and a host of specialized committees.  The number who hold office is increased by the
limits on re-eligibility of both elective and appointive offices
within general government and economic institutions.  For
example, no member of a communal assembly can be re-
elected to a second consecutive term.  This principle is applied all the way up to the level of the federal government; no
member of the Federal Assembly can be elected for a second
term to the same chamber, and no member of the Federal Executive Council is eligible for a second term unless the Federal Assembly makes a specific exception.

Also, term limitations are applied to top administrative
posts.  The senior officers of local authority administrations
are appointed for limited terms.  This contrasts with the efforts in many countries to increase the stability of local administrative officeholders and illustrates the high priority
that Yugoslav policy puts on broad participation in government
affairs and effective control of administration by the appointing
assemblies.

In summary, the two major political organizations, which
are composed of small local cells and indirectly chosen higher
units, operate in a centralized fashion and play leading ideologi
cal and organizational roles throughout society and government.
These organizations do not institutionally exercise authority ov

economic or government bodies. They seek to educate, influence, and promote unified values expressed by the socialist ideology of the nation and to establish a uniform framework of social values and goals within which decentralized administration can take place.

This chapter has outlined the general context of administration in the Zagreb urban area. The government structures involved in this administration are described in Chapter 2, and Chapter 3 analyzes intergovernmental relationships. Chapter 4 discusses the particular systems of planning and plan implementation having impact on the development of the urban area, and Chapter 5 takes a closer look at the organization for provision of four selected urban services. Finally, Chapter 6 summarizes the discernible strengths and weaknesses of the administrative system as it operates in Zagreb and the major issues of urban-government organization, and draws some comparisons with other urban areas.


## NOTES TO CHAPTER 1

1.    The term "commune" is used throughout this study to translate opcina, the uniform unit of local government, both rural and urban, throughout Yugoslavia.

2.    This modification was decided upon in the Sixth Congress of the Communist Party of Yugoslavia, held in Zagreb in 1952.

3.    Comparison of the territorial pattern of local units in 1949 and 1964 shows that the net effect of the changes has been to replace the traditional regions with district units, the traditional districts with communes, and the traditional communes and local committees with neighborhood associations. This purely territorial comparison does not take into account the changes in structure, powers, and citizen participation that have occurred in these local units.

4.    City government is organized for the nine-commune urban area, not the smaller central-city area, which is not a government unit but merely a designation for planning purposes only.

5.　The over-all densities as of the census of 1961 were 530 persons per square mile in the Zagreb District, 1,900 per square mile in the urban area of Zagreb, and 3,800 per square mile in the central city.

6.　See Stanko Žuljic: "O dnevnim kretanjima radne snage u zagrebu," Geografski Glasnik, 1957, pp. 135-47.

7.　For a detailed discussion of the geographical development of Zagreb, see Jack C. Fisher, "Urban Analysis: A Case Study of Zagreb, Yugoslavia," Annals of the Association of American Geographers, LIII, No. 1, (September, 1963).

8.　These figures were computed from data available in the Statistical Yearbook of Yugoslavia (Statistički godisnjak jugoslavije, 1964) and Statistical Survey of the City of Zagreb (Statistički pregled grada zagreba, 1962 and 1964) and in unpublished city accounts.

9.　Services include hotels and restaurants, personal service, public utilities, government administration, culture, education, health, welfare, banking, and insurance.

10.　These figures were computed from data in Statističke informacije, No. 1, 1963, and G. zavoda az statistiku grada Zagreba.

11.　According to the United Nations, Statistical Yearbook, 1962 (New York: United Nations, 1963), p. 488, national income "equals the sum of compensation of employees, income from unincorporated enterprises, rent, interest and dividends accruing to households, saving of corporations, direct taxes on corporations and general government income from property and entrepreneurship." National income in the urban area is an aggregate that represents a geographic breakdown of the national figure.

12.　Source of this data is the Statistical Institute of the City of Zagreb, "Rezultati popisa stanovnistva" (Zagreb: 1963). Both nominal and real incomes of employed persons have been rising.

13.　Employing institutions contribute a percentage of employees' salaries to various public funds, including those for education, housing, transportation, and social-welfare programs.

14.   The unemployment statistics are compiled by labor-exchange offices, which are organized on the local-government level under federal law and regulations as autonomous institutions managed by mixed councils composed of representatives of local authorities and delegates designated by trade unions and social-insurance agencies.  The category of unemployed includes all persons who applied to a labor-exchange office for employment, including young people, peasants, and housewives seeking employment for the first time as well as those who have been employed previously. Data are available in materials and yearbooks of the Institute of Statistics of Zagreb.

15.   Constitution of the Socialist Federated Republic of Yugoslavia.  Official Journal, Službeni list SFRJ, No. 14 (Belgrade:  1963), p. 263.

16.   Status saveza komunista jugoslavije  (Belgrade: 1958), p. 5.

17.   In 1966, this secretariat was provisionally replaced by a larger presidium.

18.   The hierarchical pattern of decision-making within the political organizations is not, however, repeated in governmental and administrative organizations in Yugoslavia, where lower-level bodies have independent decision-making powers in the areas of policy assigned to them, and higher control is mainly exercised in terms of supervision of legality. This system will be discussed in the following chapters.

19.   The voters' registers were brought up to date in April, 1963, and three decisions were made at that time: First, communal assemblies were thereafter to be composed of two chambers, the communal chamber and the chamber of working organizations, in conformance with the new national Constitution (The decision spelled out what proportion of the latter chamber would come from various sectors in the economy. ); second, the division of the territory of the communes for voting purposes was made; and third, voters' meeting units were defined.

# CHAPTER 2 INSTITUTIONS OF GOVERNMENT

The total output of government in the urban area of Zagreb--promulgation and enforcement of laws and regulations, expenditure of government funds, and provision of public services--engages institutions of the national government, the Republic of Croatia, the City-District of Zagreb, the nine constituent communes, and a host of independent public corporations and agencies.

In the initial phases of state socialism immediately after World War II, the various levels of government were hierarchically linked in a unitary pattern of administration within which the bureaucracy exercised major powers. The changes since 1950, particularly as formalized in the constitutions of 1953 and of 1963, have created quite a different governmental structure, in which the fundamental unit of operating administration is the commune. Enumerated powers are allocated to the federation, republics, and districts. The powers of the communes are residual; whatever is not explicitly reserved to higher tiers is presumed to fall within the responsibility of the communes.

At each tier from commune to federation, the elected assembly is the repository of public power, on which executive agencies of government are dependent, and which selects the major executive and administrative officials. The Yugoslav system of elected assemblies gives representation both to the citizen qua citizen and to members of the employed population (including self-employed and members of cooperatives). The assemblies are bicameral or multicameral, with one or more chambers elected by people working in social and economic institutions, and a general chamber elected by citizens as a whole. The assemblies of the various government tiers are organically linked by indirect elections.

Many traditional government activities have been shifted to special public corporations and agencies outside the administrative structure of general government. General-government departments have become more policy-setting, coordinating, and supervising units, with the operations undertaken by independent agencies. This represents an explicit attempt to decentralize bureaucratic authority.

There are, then, several types of institutions involved in urban administration for Zagreb. First, are the general executive bodies of government--executive councils of the federal, republic, district, and communal assemblies--all of which include members of the representative assemblies and are responsible to them for the conduct of administrative agencies financed by the assemblies.[1] Second, are the general-government administrative agencies, i.e., federal and republic secretariats, and district and communal departments, which are financed by government budgets and are responsible to the assemblies through the executive councils. Third, are public corporations, which are managed by their own workers' councils and have independent budgets, but differ from regular economic enterprises in that, because of the public-service nature of their activities, certain of their decisions are subject to approval by local assemblies. Fourth, social-management institutions are organized as independent corporations but are subject to policy boards that include representatives of the consumers or citizens served. Fifth, a special type of public agency known as a "fund" is utilized particularly for investment in functional fields. It is generally created by a local assembly, which closely defines its purposes, powers, and sources of finance. It has an independent budget but is managed by a board appointed by the local assembly. Finally, the "institute" is a special agency of government, partly supported by the government budget but organized outside the structure of general line departments.

## HIGHER-GOVERNMENT ORGANIZATION

At present, the most significant role of the national government in urban government is that of lawmaking and general-policy formulation. Highest policy-making power in the Federal Republic of Yugoslavia is vested in the Federal Assembly, which is composed of five chambers of 120 members each: the Federal Chamber, Economic Chamber, Welfare and

Health Chamber, Education and Culture Chamber, Organization and Political Chamber. Each national law is as a rule
passed by vote of two chambers, the Federal Chamber and
the chamber to whose functional fields the law is predominantly related. The Federal Assembly has three types of
lawmaking powers. First, in areas enumerated in the Constitution as of direct concern and responsibility to the federal
government, the Federal Assembly may pass "complete" and
directly enforceable laws and regulations. In addition, the
Federal Assembly passes two types of laws dealing with matters that are the primary responsibility of republic or local
authorities. "General laws" determine the principles and
policies to be followed in education and culture, health and
social welfare, and other matters in which the federation does
not pass complete laws. These general laws are not directly
enforceable but provide the policy basis for local regulation.
"Basic laws," the third type, are enforceable but are cast in
general terms and are normally supplemented by more detailed republic and local regulations.

The members of the Assembly's Federal Chamber,
which votes on every national law, include ten representatives
from each of the six republics who are elected by the general
chambers of the republic assemblies. The remaining members of the Federal Chamber are elected by communal assemblies, or groups of them, from candidates nominated by
voters' meetings (or by a minimum number of citizens). The
other four chambers of the Federal Assembly consist of candidates nominated by employed persons voting in appropriate
economic and social institutions, and elected by the communal
assemblies. After the vote is taken in communal assemblies
for representatives to republic and federal assemblies, the
candidates are submitted for ratification by popular vote. If
the candidates do not receive the majority of the popular vote,
their election by the communal assembly is voided. The role
of the Socialist Alliance and the League of Communists is
much more decisive in nominations to the Federal Assembly
than to local assemblies.

The modifications in national-government structure over
the past decade, particularly those in the Constitution of 1963,
have been designed to strengthen the role of the Assembly
vis-à-vis the executive. Members of the Assembly have the
right to initiate legislation, and the Assembly itself (the Federal Chamber plus one special chamber--the Economic

Chamber in most major matters) passes federal laws, adopts
the national plans and budgets, and supervises the work of
the administration. While most legislation still originates
with executive bodies[2], the Federal Assembly in recent years
has passed frequent resolutions that provide guidelines for
drafting measures. The Federal Chamber of the Assembly
appoints all top executive officials except the President of
Yugoslavia, who is elected by joint session of all the chambers.
Standing committees are to be organized under the 1963 Constitution to participate in legislative drafting and in supervision of the administration.

The principal executive body charged with implementing
general policies and laws adopted by the Assembly and with
coordinating government activity is the Federal Executive
Council, which is conceived of as an organ of the Assembly.
At least ten of its members, who have frequently been officials of political organizations, are elected by and from the
Federal Assembly upon the proposal of one deputy, who is
selected by the President of Yugoslavia. In addition, the
presidents of the executive councils of the six republics and
the administrative heads of national-government departments
are members by virtue of their offices. The Council serves
a term of four years, running parallel with that of the Assembly, and members are not eligible for a second term except by special vote. They may be recalled at any time.

The Executive Council submits the annual budget and
economic-development plans to the Assembly, as well as most
of its draft laws. The Federal Executive Council may issue
bylaws when so authorized by statute, and both it and government departments can issue orders and regulations in accordance with legislation.

The President of Yugoslavia is the chief of state, com-
mander of the armed forces, and representative of the country.
He promulgates Assembly laws and designates a member of it
to draw up the list of candidates for the Federal Executive
Council. In times of war, the President may issue decrees
with the force of law. If the President stays any decree or
other regulation of general political significance passed by the
Executive Council, the matter must be placed immediately before the Federal Chamber of the Assembly for decision. After

the service of President Tito, the tenure of office of the President of Yugoslavia shall be limited to two consecutive four-
year terms.

From the point of view of government for Zagreb, the
most striking fact about the federal bureaucracy is its drastic
reduction of power over the past decade, during which administrative duties have devolved upon local authorities and
certain federal functions have been vested in semi-autonomous
agencies.[3]  Prior to 1963, a general department of govern-
ment--the Federal Secretariat for Social Welfare and Communal Affairs--was responsible for matters relating to urban
development, local government, and housing.  This department was replaced by a special federal authority--the Institute
for Communal Affairs--charged with performing research and
providing general advisory services relating to local-government activities.  Recently the Institute was discontinued.  At
present, there is a Unit for Communal Affairs within the Secretariat for Health and Social Policy.  The role of the federal
secretariats relating to functional clusters of activity, such
as health and transportation, is mainly that of formulating
regulations that implement national law and supervising the
activities of lower units of government for legality and conformity to formal national-government policies.

The general administrative structure of the national government is determined by Assembly legislation, except that two
state secretariats are established by the Constitution--Defense
and Foreign Affairs.  The Federal Executive Council and the
agencies themselves, however, have important powers of administrative organization.  The Executive Council can establish subdivisions of existing institutions, and specific internal
organization is determined by agency regulations.  There are
eleven federal secretariats (in addition to the two state secretariats), one federal committee, the Federal Institute for
Economic Planning, and a number of other special authorities.
The heads of the secretariats are appointed not by the executive but by the Assembly for four-year terms, with limited
re-eligibility.

The constitutional structure of the six constituent republics of Yugoslavia (Croatia, Slovenia, Bosnia-Hercegovina,
Montenegro, Serbia, Macedonia) follows the federal model.
The Socialist Republic of Croatia--of which Zagreb is the
capital--has a five-chamber assembly elected in a manner

similar to that for the Federal Assembly.  The Croatian
Executive Council is composed entirely of persons elected by
the Assembly from its own members.  The republic government has powers of regulation over affairs within its boundaries, but its laws and other rules must conform with its own
constitution as well as with federal laws and regulations and
the federal Constitution.  Of most importance for Zagreb is
the Institute for Town Planning of the republic, responsible
to the Croatian Secretariat for Housing and Communal Affairs.

## LOCAL GOVERNMENT IN ZAGREB

The Zagreb area has a two-tier urban government consisting of the nine constituent communes and the city-district.
The nine-commune urban area is legally designated a city.
The second-tier government of Zagreb operates both as general district for the twenty-commune District of Zagreb and
as "city government"--in effect, metropolitan government--
for the nine-commune urban portion of the district.

This structure has emerged from the series of modifications in local-government organization since 1953.  The
traditional single-government unit of the City of Zagreb was
not essentially affected by the establishment in 1946 of "Bor-
ough People's Committees," which were, although legally
units of local government in their own right, never really more
than field offices of the city government.  The real change began in 1953, with the establishment of eight communes within
the city territory.  This measure, still controversial, was
designed to create smaller units in order to heighten popular
participation in and influence on local decision-making.  Beginning in 1955, the city and surrounding rural territory were
integrated into the Zagreb District on several grounds:  the
population in the rural areas was already dependent on the
city for a number of services and facilities, the administrative
expansion of the district boundaries anticipated and facilitated
the actual expansion of the urbanized area, and it would accelerate the economic and social development of the surrounding rural territory.  These two trends of expanding the district and subdividing the city resulted by the early 1960's in
the present organization of Zagreb, which gives administrative reality to a large region (the twenty-commune district),
to the metropolitan area or city, and to local communes.

## The Urban Communes

By comparison with other nations of the world, communes in Yugoslavia have extensive powers. Under the special arrangements for urban Zagreb, they remain independent units of government, but important urban functions rest with the metropolitan-level city government, unlike the normal arrangements in other parts of the country. Local-government structure entails widely shared executive powers but includes a chief administrative officer. Communes are identified by the Constitution of Yugoslavia of 1963 as the fundamental units of administration in the nation, with responsibility for administering and implementing national law as well as undertaking a broad range of activities under a general grant of powers. [5] The responsibilities of the commune as defined in the Constitution (Article 96) include: creation of material and other conditions for work and for the development of productive forces (i. e., economic and social infrastructure), regulation and coordination of the economy and social services, determination and distribution of resources (revenues) for communal requirements, coordination of individual and public interests, organization of the organs of government and of social services of common public concern, assurance of conditions for the realization of the freedom and rights of the citizens, determination of the general conditions for the discharge of the business of communal and similar organizations, safeguarding of legality and the security of the people and property, maintenance of public peace and order, and exercise of social supervision.

The general structure of communal government is determined by federal law; the territory of specific communes is defined by republic law. The basic document spelling out the details of communal organization is the charter that is adopted by the communal assembly without ratification by higher organs of government and is subject only to control by the constitutional courts as to conformity with the Constitution and laws. Within its sphere of territorial and broad functional competence, the commune prescribes its own laws, adopts social- and economic-development plans, adopts its own budget, and creates autonomous financial funds and other special agencies. The commune controls the number and specific qualifications of its personnel, which it independently hires, within prescriptions of national law.

The commune is governed by a bicameral assembly consisting of: 1) the communal chamber, elected by general franchise; and 2) the chamber of working organizations, elected by employed citizens voting in enterprises or operating institutions and by farmers organized in cooperatives. The two chambers have generally equal standing and as a rule sit together. They are elected for terms of four years, and no member can be elected for a second consecutive term. (Every second year, half the members of the assembly are replaced.) The assemblies organize committees that function as auxiliary working bodies without independent decision-making powers.

Executive responsibility is vested in executive boards of the assembly called "councils." Councils are mixed bodies appointed by the assembly from its own membership, and from citizens at large or interested nongovernment organizations. The councils are organized on the basis of one or more related functional fields. Under policies determined by the assembly, they regulate matters within their sphere of activity and issue directives that are binding upon the corresponding communal agencies. Bringing together general-government deputies and representatives of independent agencies and enterprises concerned in a given subject area, the councils undertake discussion of the general state of affairs in that category, attempt to coordinate the activities of various agencies and enterprises, both government and nongovernment, and submit proposals to the local assembly. As they usually include leading citizens and technical experts, they tend to play a large role in technically oriented fields, such as public health. The councils act not only as administrative watchdogs for the local assemblies but also as channels of communication between official policies and specialized public opinion.

The president of the communal assembly is a salaried, full-time official charged with duties of political initiative and coordination. He coordinates the work of the assembly chambers and the councils, submits agenda, signs the orders of the assembly, and countersigns the rules issued by the councils together with the president of the respective council. His contact with the communal administration is in theory through the secretary of the commune. His de facto power is considerable.

The secretary, a professional administrator, is the senior administrative officer of the communal government. He is appointed by the assembly after public competition based on merit. After a term of four years, a full vote of the assembly is required for his reappointment. Moreover, his service may be terminated at any time by a simple majority. The secretary is responsible for providing leadership and coordination of the administrative machinery, which is composed of a number of departments and their subdivisions. The department heads are responsible in matters of administrative procedure and discipline to the secretary, and in matters of substantive policy to the assembly through the appropriate council.

The administrations of the nine communes within the City of Zagreb range in size from 100 to 250 employees. Communal departments include general administration; economic affairs and labor relations; finance; inspection; building, urban and communal affairs, and housing; social services; national defense; the social-welfare center; and the public attorney and magistrate judges. The directing officers of each department are appointed by the assembly, after public competition for the post and on the recommendation of a committee for elections and appointments that includes members of the assembly and delegates from the local committee of the Socialist Alliance.

The communes in Zagreb are empowered to exercise all the general powers with which communes throughout Yugoslavia are endowed, but have tended to delegate major responsibility for urban services to the metropolitan city government.

First, the economic functions of communes include preparation of social and economic development plans in which the plans and programs of various enterprises within the communal territory are integrated, and formal supervision of all economic enterprises whose headquarters are located within the commune. Formal supervision of economic enterprises is precisely defined in national law and consists mainly of three activities: 1) commune representatives sit on the nominating committees that recommend candidates for enterprise directors; 2) the commune may guarantee bank loans to enterprises in its area; and 3) the commune oversees the legality of enterprise activity and may bring transgressions to the

courts.  As representatives of the workers in various enterprises sit in the second chamber of the communal assembly,
there is an important mechanism of interchange between
government and industry at the foundation of communal supervision and coordination of economic activities.

Second, the commune manages urban land that is publicly held, and grants rights to its use through competitive
bidding.

Third, the commune organizes public-consumption services (such as housing, water supply, public transport, cultural facilities, food supply, recreation, and entertainment).
Here the role of the communes in Zagreb has atrophied (or in
many instances has never fully developed).

Finally, the communes organize political activities:
neighborhood associations, voters' meetings, referendums,
and other mechanisms for citizen participation in government.

The voters' meetings in Zagreb periodically discuss
local-government activities and make recommendations to the
communal assembly on both policies and candidates for assembly councils.  The assemblymen must give reasons to a
meeting if its proposals are rejected.  Moreover, new special local taxes must be ratified by referendum.

Neighborhood associations in Zagreb (the "political outposts of the commune," which approximate wards) are less
important than those in rural areas, where they are village
institutions.  The commune may delegate tasks to them; for
the most part, they organize some local services such as day
nurseries, laundries, and small-park maintenance.

### The City

The City of Zagreb is a metropolitan government.  The
structure of city government consists, like that of the communes, of an assembly, its executive councils, and administrative departments headed by a secretary.  (See Chart 1.)
The city assembly, however, is multicameral and is indirectly
elected.  It consists of four chambers:  the city chamber of
120 members, the economic chamber of 50 members, the education and culture chamber of 35 members, and the welfare
and health chamber of 35 members.  The city chamber is

CHART 1

CITY ASSEMBLY OF ZAGREB
(1964)

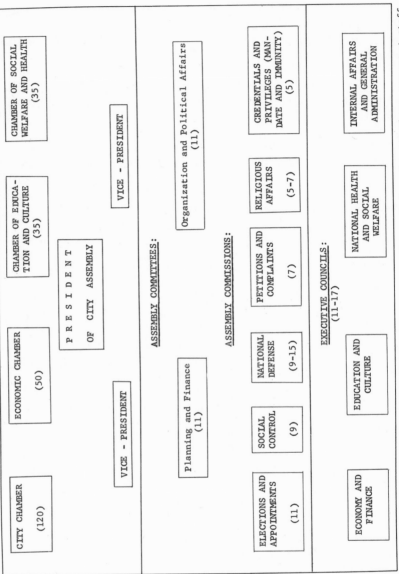

Note: Numbers in parentheses represent staff.

36

composed of deputies elected by the assemblies of all twenty
communes in the Zagreb District from their own membership. The members of the other chambers are delegated
from the chambers of working organizations of the assemblies of the nine urban communes comprising the city. [6]

The city assembly has seven standing committees:
planning and finance, organization and legislation, elections
and appointments, social control, national defense, petitions
and complaints, and religious affairs. These prepare draft
regulations and plans for action by the assembly as a whole.

The executive organs of the city government are four
councils or executive boards--economic and financial affairs,
education and culture, national health and social welfare, internal affairs and general administration--together with the
assembly president and two vice-presidents. The councils
were reorganized into their present structure during 1964,
and each includes from eleven to seventeen members, both
assemblymen and laymen. Prior to the reorganization, there
were sixteen councils, one for each major cluster of activity,
such as housing, education, work and labor relations, and
health. In addition, some chairmen of chambers of the city
assembly have exercised considerable influence and leadership in city government.

The city administration is headed by an administrative
officer--the secretary. Employees of the city administration
numbered 600 in 1964 and 300 in 1966. This is an extremely
small staff by comparison to cities of similar size in other
nations. The small and declining staff is accounted for by
functional decentralization--the shifting of operations in local
activities to special authorities and autonomous institutions.
The city government's civil-service commission was abolished
recently, as these separate authorities have been given responsibility for their own personnel management. The basic
departments of city government include general administration;
finance; economic affairs; trade and marketing; building, communal, and housing affairs; education and culture; public
health and social welfare; inspection; national defense; and internal affairs. (See Chart 2.)

CHART 2

ZAGREB CITY ADMINISTRATION
(1964)

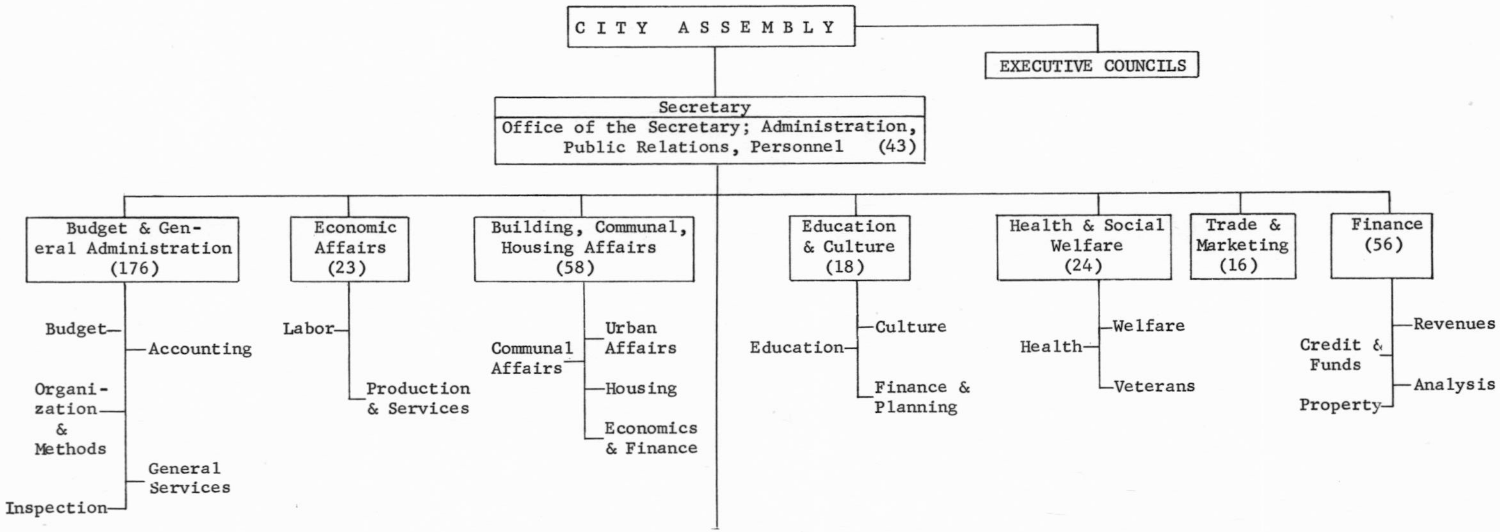

CITY ASSEMBLY

EXECUTIVE COUNCILS

Secretary
Office of the Secretary; Administration,
Public Relations, Personnel    (43)

Budget & General Administration (176)
- Budget
- Accounting
- Organization & Methods
- General Services
- Inspection

Economic Affairs (23)
- Labor
- Production & Services

Building, Communal, Housing Affairs (58)
- Communal Affairs
- Urban Affairs
- Housing
- Economics & Finance

Education & Culture (18)
- Education
- Culture
- Finance & Planning

Health & Social Welfare (24)
- Health
- Welfare
- Veterans

Trade & Marketing (16)

Finance (56)
- Credit & Funds
- Revenues
- Property
- Analysis

38

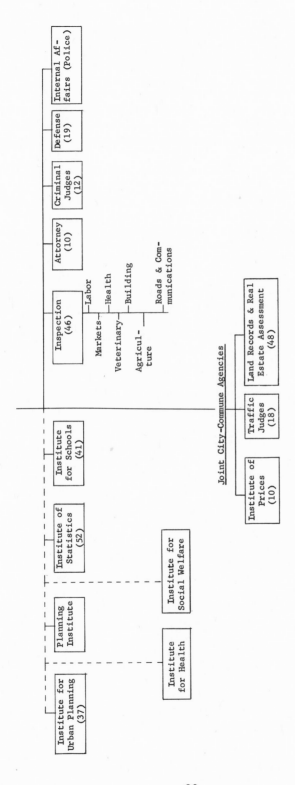

Institute for Urban Planning (37) — Planning Institute — Institute of Statistics (52) — Institute for Schools (41)

Institute for Health — Institute for Social Welfare

Inspection (46) — Attorney (10) — Criminal Judges (12) — Defense (19) — Internal Affairs (Police)

Markets — Labor — Health — Veterinary — Building — Agriculture — Roads & Communications

Joint City-Commune Agencies

Institute of Prices (10) — Traffic Judges (18) — Land Records & Real Estate Assessment (48)

Note: Numbers in parentheses represent staff. Broken lines denote coordinating powers of city government over independent institutions.

39

## Metropolitan Powers

The specific powers and responsibilities of the city-district government are enumerated in the Zagreb City Charter, which was ratified by the communal assemblies of the nine urban communes. These fall under two headings, those pertaining to its district role and those related to its special metropolitan role. Under the first heading are particularly: coordination and stimulation of the activities of the communes, preparation of the general program for economic and social development, regional land use and development planning, exercise of administrative authority conferred upon districts by federal and republic legislation, and common functions delegated to the district by the communes. The special responsibilities devolving upon the Zagreb government in its metropolitan role and applied specifically to the nine-commune urban jurisdiction include: preparation and adoption of economic and social plans, urban planning, determination and distribution of tax revenues in the urban area (normally a function of communes), legislation for the urban area in common affairs, and establishment of common public services and agencies. The Zagreb government serves both as a general district--which is an instrument through which higher governments exercise their limited perogatives of control over communes--and as an association of urban communes for metropolitan government. [7]

The city assembly legislates in all fields of concern to the urban area as a whole, but only after consultation with the communes. The expressed opinion of the communes politically influences, but does not legally bind, the city assembly. It is generally understood that in exercising all of its coordinating functions, the city will act in constant collaboration with the communes as well as with the Zagreb Chamber of Commerce and other nongovernment agencies and organizations. The city has fundamental responsibility for policy development, however, in the major areas of urban administration, particularly the development of manufacturing, crafts, trade and tourism; the supply of city markets with food; housing and construction of public utilities; schools and education, especially secondary and technical education; cultural activities, sports, and recreation; health and social welfare; police, internal affairs, and civil defense.

In addition to its legislative functions, the city exercises its coordinating responsibilities by planning. The city's planning agencies undertake both economic and physical plans for the urban area as a whole, which include development programs for all major urban services and infrastructure.

The city's most important powers are financial. The city assembly, by its own decision, divides the revenue resources in the urban area, within limits circumscribed by federal and republic law, between itself and the communes. The major sources of local revenue are taxes shared with higher levels of government, including income and business-turnover taxes. In Zagreb, the city government determines the allocation of the communal-government share. In practice, fiscal planning and management by the communes is closely coordinated by city authorities during the technical phases of budget preparation. In sessions called by the leading officers of the city (president, vice-president, and secretary), the officers of the communes and staffs of the finance departments of both city and communes hammer out the budget drafts.

## Special Authorities

An important component of urban administration in the area is a myriad of special authorities that have separate budgets and independent management, and are subject to general city-government policy and supervision in varying degrees. The trend of recent years has been to delegate to proliferating special authorities more and more of the activities of city and communal government in Zagreb in an effort to achieve functional decentralization and broaden the base of administrative decision-making. [8]

Many operations that were situated within Zagreb government and financed by the general city and commune budgets have been reorganized into semi-autonomous institutes. Many of these are staff operations--research, statistics, planning, and audit--undertaken at present by institutes and similar organizations. The Zagreb Institute for Urban Planning and the Center for Economic Development fall into this category. The latter was formed in 1966 from a merger of the Institute of Statistics and the Institute for Economic

Planning. In addition are the autonomous Institute for Schools and health and welfare agencies. Health services are the responsibility of a network of institutes, financed through the social-insurance system (by enterprise contributions) and by the communes and city, which enter into annual contracts with them. These are coordinated by a separate Zagreb Institute for the Protection of Health, which is concerned with the whole urban area and works closely with the city department of public health and social welfare.

Public corporations operate urban services, such as transport, water supply, and sanitation. They are managed by their own workers' councils and are financed in large part from user charges. Their relationship to local authorities is complex, for while the communes exercise formal supervision over the enterprises headquartered in them, the city government has, under its own charter provisions, policy and planning responsibilities in the subject areas in which these corporations are engaged. In the past, they have received local subsidies, particularly for capital investment. Urban-area physical and economic plans incorporate their work programs. Administrative departments of the city government attempt to coordinate their activities. Finally, the city assembly has approval powers over their price lists.

Schools, hospitals, and apartment houses are examples of a third type of independent agency that is subject to a policy board--such as the school board and house council, which include employee and resident representatives, respectively. These "social-management bodies" in many cases are subsidized by local authorities and coordinated by the city government.

Finally, the special funds have been organized to provide separate financing mechanisms for various functional fields. Each fund has a charter and a management board appointed by the creating assembly. The management board is in some cases responsible only for financial management of the monies in the fund. But in other instances, it is given the larger responsibility for policy-making in the field financed by the fund, within the limits of the social and economic plans and on the basis of instructions received from the assembly. In all cases, the management board has to submit a yearly financial plan of revenue and expenditures of the fund for approval by the assembly. The funds are financed by

specially earmarked taxes and fees defined by the creating
government unit.  In the Zagreb urban area are found a
school fund, public-service fund, roads fund, higher-
education fund, communal-utilities fund, children's-welfare
fund, reserve fund of economic enterprises, and fund for
covering losses in the sale of agricultural products.

## NOTES TO CHAPTER 2

1.   National and republic governments each have a
single executive council.  In communes and districts, several
specialized councils or executive boards oversee administration.  See below, page 31 and following.

2.   In practice, origination of legislative proposals by
executive bodies is common in most of the nations examined
by case studies in this series.

3.   This trend contrasts with that in many other countries, including the United States, where the growth of central-
government agencies dealing with urban matters and depart-
mentalization of central functions are found.

4.   Law on the Federal Organs of Administration, Official Journal of the Federal Republic of Yugoslavia, No. 11
(1965).

5.   The 1958 Program of the League of Communists
stated: "The commune represents the outstanding institution
of direct socialist democracy... the basic cell of self-
management of citizens in common affairs."

6.   Apportionment of seats among the communes is by
a complex formula that takes account of population, per capita
income, and employment.

7.   The city charter specifies: "The powers and duties
of the city in its functions of common interest for the narrower
urban area as a whole are performed by the city assembly
and its organs with participation and collaboration of the commune assemblies, other organs of social self-government and
citizens in voters' meetings and other forms of direct decision-
making." (Article 5:2.) The competence of the city is derived
from its legal powers "to direct and to coordinate economic

and social development, to determine and to divide the resources necessary to provide for common social needs, to
establish and to organize services, working organizations and
other organizations of common interest for that area. "
(Article 39:2. )

8.    The proliferation of special metropolitan authorities
is evident in many urban areas around the world.   Usually
this has taken place on an ad hoc basis to accommodate needs
for metropolitan services where there is no general metropolitan government.   By contrast, this phenomenon has been
systematically planned in Zagreb to implement policies of
decentralization of power and has been accompanied by
shrinking government bureaucracies.   In addition, measures
for coordination are being explicitly thought out and developed.

CHAPTER **3** INTERGOVERNMENTAL
RELATIONSHIPS

The tasks of the several levels of government in Yugoslavia overlap in subject but differ in kind.  The present allocation of powers, as has been pointed out, reflects an organized effort to strengthen local authorities and expand
their administrative role in order to counterbalance and eventually replace centralized power structures, especially the
state bureaucracy, in society.  Territorial-decentralization
measures of the Constitutions of 1953 and 1963 and of national
legislation have resulted in local authorities replacing the
national bureaucracy in operating administration over the
whole range of direct economic functions undertaken by government.  The national government has been divested of direct control and management in both productive-enterprise
and public-consumption services, including the creation of
urban infrastructure and the provision of urban services.
This contrasts distinctly with trends in other nations, where
the role of central government in urban programs is generally
growing.  The national government remains to date, however,
the major source of general regulation in Yugoslavia.  It defines the respective roles and responsibilities of basic government and economic institutions, their fundamental goals
and values, and the broad policies governing most functional
fields in which local agencies are involved.

The Constitution of Yugoslavia not only allocates governmental powers and responsibilities among the various
levels of government but also describes the proper relationships among the levels of government.  Constitutional law
provides that administrative agencies at each level are responsible to the elected assemblies at that level, not to higher
administrative units.  It requires that the relationships of
federal, republican, district, and communal agencies be
based not on hierarchy of authority but on mutual rights and
duties formally established by law.  Administrative units are

45

exhorted by the Constitution to engage in voluntary cooperation, but the document makes clear that the keystone of formal intergovernmental relations in Yugoslavia is to be statutory.


## ALLOCATION OF POWERS

### Responsibility for Urban Services

The general rule for dividing responsibilities among
levels of government is that local responsibility is assumed
in all cases where the federal or republic constitution has
not expressly proclaimed direct federal or republic responsibility. The scope of enumerated federal powers detracts
somewhat from the principle of dominant local responsibility
in public affairs. The national government has <u>exclusive
jurisdiction</u> over protection of national security, organization
of the armed forces, protection of the constitutional order
and internal security, international relations, citizenship,
foreign trade, customs, monetary policy, air traffic, international passenger traffic, and "organization of the federation
and execution of tasks and affairs for which only the federation is competent in accordance with the Constitution." Additional subjects over which the federal government may
exercise <u>direct</u> <u>authority</u> and in which it may pre-empt the
field by passage of "complete laws" and regulations include:
organization of public enterprises and the economy, property
law, credit and banking, criminal code, general administrative procedures, public security, elections and civil rights.
All major political, economic, financial, and property legislation is national. The republics--in this case, the Republic
of Croatia--have direct responsibilities in education, culture,
health, social welfare, and recreation.

Operating line agencies responsible directly to the federal or republic government can be created by statute to engage in activities within these spheres of direct responsibility,
but the legislatures have made sparing use of this alternative.
In fact, central services have shrunk rapidly while local activities have expanded. By and large, administrative agencies
and operating organizations outside the capital are under the
authority of local government.

Hence, virtually all urban-development activities and urban services are performed by agencies responsible to local authorities--the city and communes in Zagreb. Local-government functions are various and manifold, and are based on a general legal grant of powers to the local authorities to provide public services and to create the environment for productive enterprise. Thus, housing programs, water supply and sewerage, street cleaning, public transport, educational and cultural institutions, hospitals and public-health centers, recreational facilities, streets and highways, power, land development and allocation, police and fire services are all financed and provided by intra-urban agencies in Zagreb.

This arrangement makes the central and republic governments dependent upon local authorities to implement their policies. Even direct economic controls are locally administered. Thus, while the federal government has passed a great deal of legislation relating to economic enterprises, each enterprise is directly supervised by the communal assembly in Zagreb in which its headquarters are located, no matter how national in impact the business it conducts. Price increases must be reported to the chamber of working organizations of the communal assembly, and the communes exercise price control over certain retail consumer goods. Wage controls, apart from minimum-wage legislation, were recently eliminated.

In Zagreb, both city and communal agencies are involved in each major urban service.[1] Allocation of responsibilities between the two tiers of urban local government has varied more with the difficulty of the task and scope of the problem treated than with the particular service involved. Even though the communes in Zagreb are larger than municipal units in most areas of the world, it is felt that their capability to take over whole service areas, such as housing or education, is limited. In fact, the responsibilities of the urban area-wide unit in all functional categories is expanding in relation to those of the communes.

Hence, in providing urban services and shaping urban development in Zagreb, the city government has the dominant role. In fact, most urban-government activities are matters of "common concern" to the area as a whole, and meaningful "coordination" entails policy control. There are no specific rules for the precise division of many activities between

commune and city; their charters have proved sufficiently
flexible to allow for varying practical arrangements for
dealing with the urban problems encountered.  The nature of
these arrangements becomes more evident in Chapter 5,
wherein four services are examined in some detail, but some
examples may be useful at this point.

In public housing, city agencies invest in major construction; communal agencies invest in small-scale construction and repair.  Small parks and playgrounds are controlled
by communes; major ones are planned and regulated by the
city but maintained by the communes.  Fire protection is a
city service that is supplemented by voluntary fire services
in the communes.  Police is a city-wide service, although
communes have certain powers in relation to precincts in
their territory.  Water supply, transit, sewerage, and electricity are provided by public corporations operating throughout the city and subject to certain policy controls of the city
government.  But the communes in which they are headquartered exercise formal supervision, as was pointed out
in Chapter 2.  Communes operate local markets, administer
licensing bylaws, and operate social-welfare centers.

### The Roles of Government Levels

The division of powers among local authorities, republics, and the national government, then, is primarily not by
service areas but by the nature of the government processes--
operating management, financing, policy-making and regulation, and planning.  (The exceptions to this pattern are foreign
affairs and national defense.)

As administrators of the first resort, local authorities
initiate, organize, and provide operating finance for urban
services.  Although the day-to-day management of most public services is undertaken by the autonomous working organizations or public corporations, these are established by city
and commune assemblies and--because of their particularly
public service aspects--they have a closer relationship to
city authorities than do ordinary productive enterprises.  The
general administrative units of city government provide policy
guidance.  The city budget or special investment funds supplement their revenues, particularly for capital investment.
And certain classes of their decisions, such as fares and

prices, are subject to approval by the city assembly. Moreover, local governments are the responsible enforcement
agencies for national and republic laws as well as for local
regulations.

Decision-making for specific investments, as well as
for operating expenditure, is concentrated within the urban
area. Neither republic nor federal authorities are directly
involved in authorizing major investments in urban facilities
or in approving various budget categories of expenditure in
Zagreb.[2] The city and communal assemblies and management boards of the special funds and public corporations
interact in financial decision-making in the public services.
The investment programs of special authorities are integrated
into the annual investment plans of the local authorities, which
are adopted by the assemblies. Specific decisions for capital
improvements, such as an urban-renewal project, new transit route, or new schools, are submitted to the local assembly by the operating agencies or assembly executive councils.
The investment decision must be taken by the communal or
city assembly as well as by the appropriate management
board. The sources of capital for most urban services and
development projects include revenues of the operating agency
and local-government budget and special funds.

In addition, local governments can influence investment
decisions by economic enterprises that are outside the realm
of public services. Actually, there is a two-way flow of influence between major economic enterprises and local assemblies in Zagreb. All enterprise investment programs are
incorporated into local-government plans; bank loans to
enterprises are guaranteed by the communal assembly.

In general, then, specific decision-making, implementation and management, and application of the law are local-
authority roles. On the other hand, the national and republic
governments, while they cannot pass special legislation
dealing with Zagreb in particular or with a specific project,
establish by general law the framework within which local
governments act. This is more than general regulatory
power with respect to standards, for the general and basic
laws passed by the federal legislature establish the peri-
meters of most local actions. In the first instance, the
national constitution and statutes prescribe the general organization and procedures of local administration, such as

methods of planning, of personnel recruitment, and of budgeting.  National law describes the structures and duties of
communes; republic law defines the structures and duties of
the districts and establishes the boundaries of both types of
local authority.  Second, higher law governs the manner in
which public services shall be established and managed.
Federal "general" and "basic" laws and republic legislation
apply to most aspects of local-government activity.  The
Croatian government has primary regulatory powers in education, culture, health, social welfare, and recreation, and
passes regulations that carry federal law in other fields to
greater detail and specificity.[3]  The federal "basic" laws
cover such subjects as economic organizations, taxes, revenues, and distribution of social product; public loans;
water resources; commerce; transport and communications;
social planning; and social security.  "General" laws set
forth policies in all major areas of public affairs to which
local activities must conform.

Finally, planning, as shall be seen in the next chapter,
is an activity in which all levels, commune to federation,
participate and cooperate.

## Financial Resources

Like most other aspects of government, the organization
of public finance is undergoing a major change in Yugoslavia.
The most important factor in administrative decentralization
is reduction of the proportion of national income that is channeled through the central government.  This reduction has
been effected both by increasing local-government revenues
in relation to national-government revenues and by increasing
the percentage of profits that enterprises retain to reallocate
directly.  In recent years, the percentage of gross national
income channeled through central agencies has been reduced
from 70 per cent and is rapidly approaching the government's
goal of 29 per cent.

The fundamental changes in the fiscal and economic
system have naturally not been without problems, which have
given rise to some oscillation in local fiscal powers since
1953.  But the net trend has been toward the expansion of
local fiscal powers.  By 1963, approximately 57 per cent of
all general-government expenditure was made by the national
government and almost one tenth of this national outlay was

in grants to the republics. (See Table 3.) Approximately
one third of the general expenditure was that of districts and
communes. This is a sizable increase over 1951, when
local budgets accounted for 12.5 per cent of all government
budgets. Local finance is far greater, however, than these
figures would indicate, for the general budgets from which
they are derived do not include profits of public but self-
managed enterprises and expenditures of public services financed by fares and user fees, earmarked taxes, and special
funds. Total expenditures by special funds alone, at all levels,
was 343 billion dinars in 1963.

TABLE 3

General-Government Expenditures in Yugoslavia
(billion dinars)*

|                                           | 1961 | 1962 | 1963 |
|-------------------------------------------|------|------|------|
| National government:                      | 569  | 627  | 632  |
| Of which, grants to republics             | 35   | 47   | 60   |
| Republic governments:                     | 111  | 122  | 123  |
| Of which, grants to local governments     | 17   | 20   | 30   |
| Districts                                 |      | 101  | 97   |
|                                           | 299  |      |      |
| Communes                                  |      | 242  | 248  |
| Total                                     | 979  | 1,092| 1,100|

* The inflationary index for these years, based on retail
prices in a theoretical budget for an average four-member
family, is: 1961, 1,000; 1962, 1,102; 1963, 1,161.

The growth rate of nationwide local-authority expenditures in recent years exceeds that of republic and national-government expenditures, but over-all, growth of government expenditures is not significant when corrected for inflation. Expenditure by local governments (the city and nine communes) within the Zagreb urban area, however, is growing far faster than local-government expenditure in the nation as a whole.   And the relative fiscal role of the city in the urban area has expanded, as the following figures show:

TABLE 4

Local-Government Expenditures in the Zagreb Urban Area
(million dinars)

|          | 1960 | 1961 | 1962 | 1963 | 1964 |
|----------|------|------|------|------|------|
| City*    | 6,482 | 9,215 | 9,765 | 16,157 | 16,148 |
| Communes | 7,132 | 11,837 | 12,888 | 12,104 | 13,592 |
| Total    | 13,614 | 21,052 | 22,653 | 28,261 | 29,740** |

* About half the city expenditures shown are allocated by the city budget and half by special funds.
** This total of 29,740 million dinars is equal to 21,116 million dinars at 1960 prices.

The uneven expansion rates reflect governmental decisions on budgets and allocations of national revenue.

Local-government budgets and special funds are important sources of public capital investment.  In 1964, local governments provided 21 per cent of all capital investment in the nation; independent enterprises provided 26 per cent; and other local sources, 8 per cent. [4]  Between 1958 and 1963, local investment funds doubled.  In Zagreb, their finances are derived from special local tax revenues and service-user charges.

Whereas almost all investment in the nation was directly controlled by the national government in the first five-year-plan period (1945-49) after the war, by 1963 less than a quarter of investment was directly made by the federal government. The central investment fund of the national government provides for large-scale planned projects and general borrowing by enterprises, but it is not a significant source of investment in urban services and development in Zagreb. Federal influence over investment is indirect, through tax allocations and financial laws; through political organizations, trade unions, and economic chambers.

Thus, the city and communes of Zagreb control the major share of governmental expenditure in the area. Moreover, they are not dependent for their revenue sources on higher-government grants. The Republic of Croatia has not received federal grants in recent years, and local governments in the Zagreb urban area received neither republic nor federal grants.[5] On the other hand, a substantial proportion of local revenues in Zagreb (70 per cent) is derived from shared taxes collected by the communes for all levels of government. These include personal-income and business-turnover taxes. The division of these common sources of revenue starts at the center and moves downward, so that each government may decide how much to take and how much to leave to lower levels. Thus, the federal government decides what proportion shall be allocated to all lower tiers together, and at the other end of the ladder the city authorities decide what proportion of what is left to Zagreb shall be allocated to the nine communes. City authorities also decide on the division of revenues between certain city and commune investment funds in Zagreb. Annual fiscal laws through 1964 guaranteed that at least 29 per cent of the shared taxes would be returned to local authorities. Since then, they have not mentioned any guarantee.

Inherent in this system is a strong mode of control by higher government over the general scope of local-authority capabilities and latitude for action. Traditionally, the complaint has been voiced in Zagreb that federal and republic governments take too much tax income from the area. However, the city revenue has been increasing with its territory, population size, and economic development. Furthermore, the issue is mitigated by the tendency of recent years to assign each level of government its own sources of additional revenue. Revenue sources must be authorized by federal law, but the decision to levy permitted extra taxes is local. At present, the city and communes can levy their own taxes

on income, property, and business turnover to supplement
shared revenues, but maximum rates for these local taxes
are prescribed by federal law in order to preserve the balance
of the economic system and to minimize tax inequities from
area to area. The following table shows the percentage of
general revenues of the city and communes of Zagreb in 1963
by source:

TABLE 5

General-Government Revenue Sources*
(Percentages in 1963)

|  | City | Nine Communes | Total |
|---|---|---|---|
| 1. Taxes shared with republic and national governments (personal income, business turnover, and others) | 78. 6 | 60. 8 | 69. 5 |
| 2. Additional taxes levied by local government (income, property, and business turnover) | 10. 4 | 32. 5 | 21. 6 |
| 3. Transfer from reserve funds and previous budgets | 5. 8 | 5. 6 | 5. 7 |
| 4. Stamp duties | 4. 3 | . 1 | 2. 2 |
| 5. Income of government agencies | . 9 | . 9 | . 9 |
| 6. Grants by city to communes** |  | . 06 |  |

* The figures exclude revenues of special funds and public
corporations from operating income and earmarked local
taxes.
** These grants are made during the fiscal year to adapt the
division of revenues to unforeseen circumstances.

City authorities complain that the republic government,
in delegating to the city new responsibilities for implementing

higher law and regulations, often falls short of its constitutional duty to compensate the city assembly for increased
expenditure.  Zagreb has not yet put its case to legal test
in the constitutional courts.

In summary, substantial economic resources are handled locally in Zagreb, giving commune and particularly city
authorities meaningful decision-making powers.  Although
higher governments control generally the allocation of revenues, the share of local authorities has expanded rapidly
with the increase in local responsibility.  The major problems of the local financial system at present within the urban
area are threefold:

First, the division of revenue by the metropolitan city
between itself and the communes is a matter for continuing
debate between city and commune officials; the relative
amount of city revenues are expanding with the growth of
metropolitan services and activities.

Second, financial-decentralization measures entailing
a host of public corporations and investment funds, each with
a separate budget, create problems of fiscal planning and
coordination in the opinion of some local officials.  The general city budget shows payments to these institutions made
under contracts for special services or under subsidy arrangements, but it does not reflect  the institutions' expenditure from their own revenues.

Third, some problems concerning local tax procedures
have been encountered.  Whether the basis for tax assessment
should be the place where the taxpayer lives or the place
where he works has been the subject of some debate, for example.  The earlier Yugoslav system of taxation, which put
the preponderant accent on taxes paid by enterprises, favored
tax assessment on the individual by place of work.  But in
Zagreb, where people often live in one commune and work in
another, this procedure came to be considered unfair because it increased the revenues of the communes in which
factories and other economic enterprises were located and
left the poorer residential communes impoverished.  Emphasis
is shifting within the general Yugoslav tax system to taxes
paid by the individual, and the city switched in 1963 to assessment of taxes according to the domicile of the payee.
This solution creates another technical problem, however,

for the question arises as to whether the peasant who is becoming an industrial worker, living in a rented room in Zagreb, and returning to his rural home on weekends, is domi-
ciled for tax purposes in one place or the other.  A final
problem confronting Zagreb finance officials is the federal
government's recently liberalized taxation policy toward private craftsmen.  The private entrepreneur in a craft shop
has traditionally flourished in Zagreb, providing an abundant
source for local revenue collectors.  In order to stem a de-
cline in craft activity that was perhaps in part induced by
overtaxation, the Federal Assembly restricted the power of
local governments to tax craftsmen, thus diminishing an important source of revenue for local units within Zagreb.

## INTERGOVERNMENTAL CONTROLS

Each level of government in Yugoslavia within its sphere
of powers is administratively autonomous, so that federal and
republic agencies have no direct authority over city and communal officials.  Communal and city agencies are responsible,
horizontally, to the elected assembly through the appropriate
executive council and the secretary.  This is a complete re-
versal of the system in force immediately after World War II,
when vertical lines of authority between local and central
agencies in each functional field were strong.  The local education department, for example, acted on the basis of directives from the republic education department, which received
instructions from a federal committee.  At present, higher
governments do not have positive approval powers over local
decisions.  The city and communes vote their budgets, pass
their laws, adopt economic- and physical-development plans,
and (with some exceptions for the city) establish special funds
and agencies without higher ratification.

### Personnel

Control over personnel is vested in each government
unit, although general regulations are embodied in federal
law.  Senior executives, such as the secretary and department heads, are appointed by the assemblies, and other administrative posts are filled by personnel offices in both the
city and the communes.  Public competition is mandatory by
law for all administrative posts.

Yet another aspect of the movement toward decentralization and individual and group self-government in Yugoslavia has been the shifting of personnel decisions to local authorities and, further, to employees themselves in operating agencies. Central personnel functions with respect to local authorities have been reduced to, first, general regulation of work conditions, minimum wage and salary scales, and types of competitive selection procedures; and second, guidance and technical aid for recruitment, examination, and personnel policy formulation.

Recently, elected employee councils have been established in each local agency. These councils share with the agency head power to adopt internal job organization and salary plans. Disagreements between them and the agency head are to be submitted to the local assembly. In the city budget, an agency's budget is now provided by a lump-sum entry, which is allocated internally by the employee council and agency head. (A similar system has been instituted within republic and federal governments.)

In the short time that this system has been in effect, resultant decisions have not differed significantly from those that were embodied in laws and budgets. Salaries tend to correspond to type of work and training needed for it, length of service, and performance. Some differentials in salaries for comparable work in different agencies and uncertainty by employees as to their rights have emerged as negative consequences in the early stages of the system.

Both the city and the communes finance training for specialized personnel by scholarships. These students are then obligated to work for the city administration at least the number of years that they held the scholarship. [6] In-service training is provided by the city in several ways, including formal study at universities with full pay. There are, moreover, several continuing training programs for local-government staff conducted by national and republic institutions. The Federal Institute of Public Administration organizes seminars for teachers of administration, prepares curriculum materials, and engages in research. Higher schools of public administration are situated throughout the country and provide two-year college courses in the field. There are a number of secondary schools of public administration as well.

In Zagreb, the Advanced School of Public Administration of-
fers a three-year graduate course. Its graduates become
secretaries of communes, heads of departments, and other
senior officers throughout the republic and nation. Finally,
workers' schools provide limited technical and administrative
training.

## Legal Supervision

The main instrument of control over local authorities
that the national government possesses is its lawmaking
power. There is a hierarchy of statutory law, with the law
of each level binding upon the authorities of the level below
and taking precedence over lower legislation. Local lawmaking is restricted only by existing central legislation.

Particular local activities are supervised by higher
agencies in terms of legality. This supervision is not discretionary ("contrôle d'opportunité" as a rule does not exist
in the Yugoslav system). Particular illegal decisions taken
by local-government departments can be reversed by higher-
government departments if they relate to implementation of
higher-government responsibilities, such as administration
of federal taxes by local finance departments. Illegal decisions of this type by local legislative and executive organs
are similarly subject to legal control by higher representative and executive bodies. Local laws and regulations can
be overturned, however, only by going before the constitutional courts and showing them to conflict with higher law.
Pending decision by the courts, the Croatian Executive Council or Federal Executive Council can stay the enforcement of
general measures of communal or city assemblies. Similarly, the communal assemblies can stay, pending judicial
decision, enforcement of general decisions by autonomous
organizations and enterprises headquartered in their territory if they find these decisions at variance with the constitution or law.

Judicial review over intergovernmental controls is new,
for the Constitutional Court of Yugoslavia was established by
the 1963 Constitution. The procedure is designed to replace
administrative supervision with legal supervision, and to
establish law rather than discretionary authority as the foundation of intergovernmental relationships.

The actions of local authorities that are essentially enforcement of national and republic law rather than their own
undertakings are subject to somewhat stronger administrative
control. With respect to implementation of higher law, the
rights of federal and republic executive and administrative
bodies over city and commune departments and the duties of
the latter are determined by statute. Central agencies can
issue binding instructions to the local administration on how
enforcement is to be handled generally. Hence, the inspection services--financial, sanitary, building, market, labor
relations, and safety, etc. --(which are organized as city
and communal services with republic and federal counterparts)
operate in more centralized fashion than other branches of
administration, because they function mainly as agents for
enforcing central regulations. If local authorities fail to perform their legal duties of enforcement, central agencies are
empowered to do so themselves, an exception to the general
rule of "no central administration without local control. "

The Zagreb police are directly responsible to the city
department of internal affairs. While the size of the force is
determined by joint decision of the city assembly and the
Croatian secretary of internal affairs, and police salaries
are paid by the republic, there are no separate republic or
federal police.

## Fiscal Control

Fiscal control in Yugoslavia is achieved by a network
of special agencies outside the general-government structure.
National-government authorities do not audit local accounts.
Rather, fiscal supervision is exercised by republic branches
of the National Bank, and particularly the Social Accounting
Service, which records and controls transactions dealing with
public property and business. The service in Croatia is
headed by an appointed director-general, who operates according to federal statute and reports annually to both federal
and republic assemblies. Financial transactions of public
enterprises, institutions, and local governments are executed
through the National Bank branch, allowing for running current audit. Inspectors of the Accounting Service check on the
legality and regularity of these transactions. The service
can refuse to honor irregular orders for payment or can block
a government account that does not conform to budget regulations, pending administrative law proceedings.

Behavior of the Intergovernmental System

On balance, local governments in the Zagreb area play
a broader role in urban administration relative to central
authorities than those in most other nations.  At the same
time, central powers are adequate to assure that national
policies are followed and that legality and regularity are respected.  While the wide enumeration of higher-government
responsibilities somewhat reduces the significance of the
constitutional mandate that all other matters are the province
of local authorities, the national and republic governments
have chosen to become dependent upon local units for im-
plementating most of their laws and policies.  This arrangement involves a two-way dependency, however, because of
the more stringent supervision by higher government of
these local-enforcement activities.

Lack of technical assistance and guidance by central
authorities to local units with rapidly expanding responsibilities, which arise from economic development and urbanization as well as from modification in the governmental
system, is at present a more pressing problem in the nation
than overpowering central authority.  This problem is not
serious in Zagreb, however, which has relatively high governmental capabilities as a large urban center with a metropolitan government and skilled human resources.

In summary, formal decision-making powers are divided
as follows:  Local authorities in Zagreb decide what to do
within a wide range of possibilities allowable under federal
and republic law (e. g. , to create a new transit route, to develop a new city center, to construct so many housing units
in a given year).  Federal law, supplemented by republic law,
predetermines how they do things (e. g. , the manner in which
they finance investments, the type of organizations that shall
undertake and manage them, administrative procedures,
safety and health standards).  Furthermore, national philo-
sophies and the political organizations influence both the
"what" and "how" decisions.  For example, the design of new
sections of the city follows city planning theory  which is generally accepted throughout the nation.  And shifting the burden
of housing investment to nongovernment agencies follows
national policy.

The system of broad policy and legal controls does not
entail intense day-to-day administrative supervision or approval.  Each important project proposal and management
decision may be authorized within the urban area.  While
the decisions must take cognizance of controlling laws and
policies, the specific decision-making process is intra-urban
in Zagreb.  The processes of project design, debate, and
authorization involve communication among city, communes,
public corporations, and local interests rather than negotiation and communication between local and higher governments.  Hence, most of the problems of coordination and
intergovernmental relationships in Zagreb are intra-urban.

Intergovernmental mechanisms other than administrative hierarchy operate in Zagreb to produce a modicum of
harmony between local decisions and national and republic
interests.  Apart from the legal system, the centralized
political process has this effect.  The hierarchically organized League of Communists and Socialist Alliance form nongovernmental ties between different territorial levels.  The
frequent vertical contacts between the committees of these
organizations facilitate policy coordination and hence make
possible greater formal decentralization.  Although
they refrain as a rule from direct interference in the day-to-
day conduct of government, political organizations are by far
the most influential participants in local decision-making.
Their influence is exerted both by organizational expression
of opinion given publicly or in consultation with local authorities, and by their membership participating in communal and
city organs of government.

In addition, the indirect election of assemblies above
the commune level and resultant links between communal,
district, republic, and federal assemblies, strengthens
coordinative tendencies.  Finally, the plans of each level of
government are closely linked and mutually related, but this
is the subject of the next chapter.

## NOTES TO CHAPTER 3

1.   Local powers that elsewhere in Yugoslavia are communal powers, are shared in Zagreb by the communes and the city.

2.   This is unusual among the cases studied in this series.   The independence in financial (both current and capital) decision-making of local authorities in Zagreb marks the system of urban administration there as more decentralized than any other examined.

3.   The republics can regulate matters reserved for federal "complete" laws only when there is no federal legislation in the field or when federal law explicitly confers that power on them.   The republics supplement federal "basic" and "general" laws with more specific measures; in fact, general laws are not enforceable without such supplementary legislation.

4.   These figures are computed from data in Bilten jugoslavenske investicione banke (Bulletin of the Yugoslav Investment Bank), No. 1 (1966).

5.   Communes unable to finance the functions for which they are responsible in Yugoslavia are eligible for subsidies paid by the central government.   The selective importance of this indirect means of control elsewhere than Zagreb is demonstrated by the following figures:

| Number of Communes | Level of Subsidy (1962) (million dinars) |
|---|---|
| 23 | Over 130 |
| 18 | 90-120 |
| 53 | 60-90 |
| 91 | 30-60 |
| 82 | 10-30 |
| 46 | Less than 10 |
| 264 | No subsidy |

6.   Active recruitment of young people into public service is unusual among urban areas examined in this series

and has proved a useful response to common personnel problems associated with advancing complexity and specialization in urban government.

| CHAPTER | 4 | PLANNING AND PLAN |
|---|---|---|

CHAPTER 4 PLANNING AND PLAN
IMPLEMENTATION

Like other aspects of government, planning in Yugoslavia has moved away from the centralized system instituted immediately after World War II, when detailed economic decisions were embodied in the national plans and enforced by administrative agencies. Currently, Yugoslavia utilizes a system of interlocking general plans prepared at each major governmental level, building up from the plans of individual enterprises and organizations. Planning theory there differs considerably from that of other socialist systems in that plans are designed as coordinative policy guideposts, rather than controlling documents encompassing specific decisions on sectoral investment and economic transfers. Workers'-council management of enterprises has removed detailed decision-making on production, investment, and operations from formal government plans to operating management. Further liberalization of the economic system in 1965 was accompanied by further loosening of the planning system.

Nevertheless, physical urban plans and economic and social plans are major mechanisms of regulation and coordination in Yugoslav administration. By involving operating agencies, communes, districts, republics, and the federal authorities in the preparation of interlocking plans of increasing scope and decreasing specificity, an attempt is made to develop an intergovernmental consensus on goals and to lay a policy foundation that will enable the diverse units engaged in a pluralistic administrative system to operate in complementary fashion. The plans themselves are not directly binding on operating authorities, but the involvement of these authorities as well as a large segment of the public in plan preparation, together with the close integration of plans with budgets and regulatory measures, strengthens the potential for plan implementation.

## THE NATIONAL PLANNING SYSTEM

The institutional framework for planning in Yugoslavia is designed to produce two distinct types of plans: first, economic and social plans; and second, physical urban plans.

Economic plans have been prepared both annually and for seven-year periods. (Earlier, five-year periods were used.) Since 1957, the national plans (for 1957-60 and 1961-65) have been not operational programs but rather general-goal frameworks. The national plans have specified rates of economic expansion, and allocation of resources by major category (for example, government budgets, personal consumption, productive investment). Up to 1965, these were elaborated in annual plans. The national plans are prepared by the Federal Planning Institute, which operated under the supervision of the Federal Economic Secretariat until 1965, when this secretariat was abolished. Currently, the director of the Institute sits on the Federal Executive Council.

Local plans do not merely implement higher plans, for they are independently prepared and add their own programs for investment of local resources. On the other hand, they are bound by the Constitution to remain within the regulatory framework of higher plans. This principle is enforceable, however, only in so far as legal regulations adopted concurrently with the higher plans are enforceable as law. Annual economic and social plans (entitled merely "social plans") and a seven-year plan have been drafted by local planning authorities in close collaboration with the republic planning agency, even though there is no legal compulsion for the local agencies to conform to higher opinions. Local plans do not require administrative or legislative approval by higher authorities. The plans of the republics are for the most part coordinative documents; they embody fewer new investment programs than national or local plans.

This articulated system of planning operates so that while lower plans elaborate higher plans in greater detail, higher plans are based on data and proposals originating in large part with local planning agencies. The Federal Planning Institute begins by preparing estimates of national income in major categories and outlining general targets for the production of capital goods, consumer products, etc.

Investment targets for both productive enterprise and public
facilities are outlined.  Production targets are set for essential key materials only.  The data with which the Federal
Planning Institute works at this stage are the estimates provided by local-government units, enterprises, and the economic chambers.

In the second stage, the draft plans of enterprises are
incorporated in both commune and economic-chamber plans,
while the commune plans are incorporated into district and
finally republic plans, which are forwarded to the Federal
Planning Institute.  After the federal plan is completed, local
planning agencies reconsider and further elaborate their own
plans.  Throughout the process, planning officials at all
levels engage in intense negotiation and consultation, during
which there is considerable give and take.  While the national
plan determines the general amount of capital available for
borrowing from the national banking system, specific capital
investments are for the most part determined by local plans.
The relative importance of local tax and other funds for investment in urban services and facilities gives significant
power to the local planners.  The federal government relies
on influencing local economic allocations through the statutory
measures dealing with direct federal investment; federally
determined taxes and interest rates; and wage, price, and
foreign-trade regulations.  The federal plan is adopted by the
federal legislature, but its production and investment targets
are not directly enforceable nor are they assigned to particular enterprises or units of government.  The entire system
of plans, from federation to commune, regulates the economic
and social development of the nation.  The expressed aims
of planning are to achieve harmonious development, to equalize
conditions of work and income, to define the criteria for distribution of social product, and to stimulate distribution of
income according to work.

Direct responsibility for physical urban planning lies
with the communes and cities in Yugoslavia, and that for regional planning with republic agencies.  Urbanization has for
nearly twenty years been regarded by the national government
as a necessary concomitant to industrialization.  Planning of
urban development has been regulated by federal legislation
since 1949, and local urban-planning institutes are established according to federal law.  The Unit for Communal Affairs in the Federal Secretariat for Health and Social Policy

provides technical assistance and advice in urban-planning
matters and supervises implementation of national laws relating to urban development.  Urban plans, however, do not
require approval by higher-government levels, and efforts to
coordinate economic and social plans with urban plans are
concentrated at the city and regional levels.

## PLANNING FOR ZAGREB

Following the national pattern, two types of multifunc-
tional plans are prepared in the Zagreb urban area:  economic
and social plans, and urban plans.  The first have been prepared by the "planning institutes" and the second by the "institutes for urban planning. " In 1965, the Zagreb Planning
Institute was merged with the Institute of Statistics to form
the Center for Economic Development, an autonomous organization.  In addition, although they are not planning agencies
in the technical sense, local assemblies, workers' councils
in public corporations, and the Zagreb Institute for Public
Health Protection and Institute for Social Welfare have important planning functions.

### Economic and Social Planning

The City of Zagreb and two of the constituent communes
have established economic planning agencies.  In the other
communes of the urban area, similar functions are performed
by general units of communal administration.  The city agency
includes three substantive divisions:  sectoral planning (dealing
with material and financial balances, income, investment,
consumption, prices and market, labor force, social services,
methodology of planning, and analysis of plan implementation);
functional planning (dealing with manufacturing, agriculture,
forestry, building, transportation, trade, catering and tourism, crafts, housing, and local services); and regional planning (dealing with territorial coordination and the harmonizing
of sectoral and functional planning from the point of view of
regional development).

Prior to 1965, directors of planning institutes were
appointed by the respective communal or city assembly, and
were responsible in matters of policy to the assembly, and
in matters of administrative procedure to the secretary of
the city or commune.  Currently, the centers of economic

development, which have replaced the planning institutes, are managed by directors appointed by a council of employees, as normal in autonomous organizations.

The Institute for the Protection of Health of the City of Zagreb and the Institute for Social Welfare of the City of Zagreb, which were created by the city assembly, undertake social planning in close collaboration with the planning agencies, with a view to developing and strengthening social services and adapting them to the needs of rapid urban growth. Their own plans and proposals are incorporated into the general social and economic plans.

Through 1965, annual social and economic plans for Metropolitan Zagreb were prepared by the planning institutes. The annual plans for the city were adopted by the assembly. Regulatory measures accompanying them were binding upon the communes and working organizations. Annual plans are no longer required, however. Instead, for 1966 the Zagreb Center for Economic Development issued a document analyzing "Results of the Development of the City of Zagreb in 1965 and Forecasts for 1966."

A Seven-Year Plan of Economic and Social Development for the City of Zagreb (1964-70) has been under discussion since 1964, but by the time it was adopted, its coverage was reduced to five years. A major issue underlying the delay concerned the extent of central control over the economy. This was resolved in favor of liberalization by the Eighth Congress of the League of Communists during 1964 and by measures passed during 1965 that were generally labeled "economic reform." A plan for the rest of the period (1966-70) was adopted in late 1966. It includes programs for urban facilities such as transportation, water supply, and housing.

The annual plans did include investment policies for the major categories of urban services and urban infrastructure. For example, annual programs of housing construction developed by the housing investment agencies were constituent parts of the commune and city plans. Thus, the housing programs of various organizations were coordinated by and formed a part of the plan documents prepared by the city and commune planning institutes and adopted by the respective assemblies.

Formally, planning procedures begin in Zagreb when
the planning agency of the city submits to all communal assemblies and to the Chamber of Commerce statistical and
analytical surveys of development during the past planning
period.  The surveys are prepared with the collaboration of
other departments and agencies of the city administration and
utilize data gathered by the network of statistical services. [1]

The communal assemblies and the Chamber of Commerce
discuss general problems of development in the coming planning period on the basis of the survey presented to them, and
they adopt policy statements on the general lines to be followed
in preparing the new plan.  These policy statements are then
discussed by the city assembly, which in its turn adopts a
resolution on the basic orientation of the new plan.  Armed
with this policy foundation, the planning agency prepares a
first draft of the city plan.  This draft is submitted to the
communal assemblies, the Chamber of Commerce, and other
autonomous organizations and agencies.  Meanwhile, public
discussion of the draft is organized in neighborhood councils
and voters' meetings.  Suggestions and criticisms offered by
these various groups are then considered, together with the
draft plan, by the communal assemblies.  The next step is
discussion of the draft and proposals in the Committee for
Planning and Finance of the city assembly, followed by review
and adoption by the full city assembly.  Thereafter, ratification by two thirds of the urban communes is required to
give the plan official status.  Throughout this process, the
Zagreb planning agency has maintained constant consultation
with the Planning Institute of the Republic of Croatia to harmonize the contents of the city plans with republic and national economic plans.

Area-wide planning is a function specifically assigned
to the city government in its coordinating role, but the communes of Zagreb did prepare their own annual social and
economic plans, which incorporated the plans of all economic
enterprises and public-service corporations headquartered
in the communal territory.  Communal estimates and proposals have formed part of the raw material of the city planning operation, and in turn the plans of the communes must
move within the framework of the city plan.

The division of planning responsibility between communes and city has been a source of problems, particularly in

that the plans and projections of enterprises and public-
service corporations that operate city-wide are channeled throug
the commune in which they are headquartered. The commune
planning authorities naturally tend to advocate the interests
of their particular commune, and conflicts of interest with
city-wide planning goals are subject to frequent negotiation
and debate. Resolution of such conflicts ultimately must come
in the political decision-making process, particularly in the
city assembly. The plans of urban communes within Zagreb
have been far more strictly and narrowly circumscribed by
the city plan than are the planning activities of rural communes by a district development program.

Throughout these planning processes, the role of enterprises, public-service organizations, and the public looms
large. The materials of which communal plans are constructed are the plans of the individual enterprises, and public-
service segments of the city plan are worked out by the operating agencies in conjunction with the planning agency. Consultation with public groups and the Chamber of Commerce,
in which economic enterprises are associated, is built into
the plan-approval process at both the commune and city levels.
Considerable discussion of economic and social plans by local
experts is carried in the press as well as in local professional
journals.

The importance of investment planning for Zagreb is
underscored by the fact that decision-making with respect to
investment is fragmented among public corporations and
autonomous funds. The process of submitting, discussing,
and approving the economic plans, involving the plethora of
operating agencies at both the commune and the city levels,
is highly complex and somewhat lengthy, but is useful, given
the degree of administrative decentralization that must be
made compatible with coordinated metropolitan development.

### Urban Planning in Zagreb

The Zagreb Institute for Urban Planning and the institutes for urban planning of two of the constituent communes
were created by the respective local-government assemblies
and vested with responsibility for urban and regional land-use
planning. [2] These institutes are organized into two substantive
divisions, one for urban analysis, another for urban planning.
Their duties include technical land-use planning, determination

of the most advantageous location for industrial and other
construction, preservation of historical sites and cultural
monuments, and long-range planning of urban services
needed for new residential quarters. The institutes for urban planning are headed by directors appointed by local
executive councils. The city institute has undertaken general survey and research work including, for example, a
survey of transportation, a compilation of old plans for the
City of Zagreb, and a plan for developing South Zagreb. Its
main function, however, is to prepare long-range urban plans
for the area.

Institutes for urban planning in two communes
undertake local zoning and "micro-planning" of blocks
or neighborhoods. They are supposed to work within
the framework of the general city plan but have been
able to assert considerable independence from the city in
pursuing narrower communal interests.

The formal urban-planning process in Zagreb includes
three stages: first, preparation of the urban program (completed in 1963); second, preparation of a thirty-year general
urban plan; and third, preparation of a detailed program for
implementing the general urban plan. A draft of the urban
program is prepared by the Zagreb Institute for Urban Planning and is submitted to a plethora of organizations, including:
the communal assemblies; neighborhood associations; operating agencies; the Chamber of Commerce; Republic of
Croatia secretariats of national defense, of transport, and of
urban, housing, and communal affairs; and the republic and
city's institutes for protection of historical monuments and
economic planning agencies. All criticism and suggestions
from both public groups and republic authorities are sifted
by the city institute. They are submitted, together with a
revised program, to the city assembly. Before the city assembly can approve the program, all suggestions and criticisms forwarded by the communes, organizations and enterprises, or individual citizens, must be discussed by the assembly and a decision taken on them. Only then can the program be put to a vote.

The same procedure is followed in the second and third
stages, that is, with the general urban plan and with the detailed program for implementation of the general urban plan.
There is an additional requirement, however--that the general

urban plan, after being passed by simple majority in the city
assembly, be ratified by two thirds of the communes. After
ratification, the urban plan is legally binding on communal
governments and operating organizations.

In general, urban planning elicits intense interest from
the press, public, and various enterprises and nongovernment organizations. Objections by voters' meetings, neighborhood councils, and communal units have, when they did
not challenge the basic thrust, caused alterations in draft
plans and programs. Approval of a binding urban plan was
stalemated by unresolved conflicts between 1953 and 1966.

The history of urban planning has been spotty in Zagreb.
Severe problems with respect to roads and health stimulated
preparation of a regulatory plan in 1936, but the major portion of the urban center had already developed. Being approved on the eve of the war, most of this plan was never
carried out. After the liberation, the areas surrounding the
city that were linked to it economically and socially became
administrative parts of it with the establishment of the present metropolitan-scale city government. The new urban
plan, which was prepared by the city institute, took into account present and future problems of the city and its sur-
roundings, as well as the position of Zagreb in the larger region and republic. The latter consideration was dealt with
in consultation with republic planning authorities and on the
basis of federal policy. Adoption of the plan, first presented
to the city assembly in 1953, was delayed primarily because
of controversy over the routing and location of railway lines
and stations. (See Chapter 5.) The approved urban program,
however, was treated as a master plan, with which city
agencies voluntarily harmonized their development decisions,
pending approval of a binding general plan and urban program,
which finally was obtained in 1966.

Moreover, the city assembly had given legal force to
some aspects of the draft plan by passing appropriate regulations and authorizations.

The adopted program and plan, projecting a doubled
population of 1,000,000 in thirty years, contemplate development programs for all major urban services and facilities in
the context of land-use designs. They lay down the general
lines along which the urban area is expected to develop.

The documents propose to check unplanned longitudinal east-
west expansion. A new urban center is being created in
South Zagreb on the Sava River. Its design is based on city-
planning theory in Yugoslavia, which posits a city center as
an administrative and cultural complex but would disperse
social and commercial facilities throughout the city in standardized neighborhood units. Neighborhood units are being
established around the new center. Land-use projections of
the plan proposed to reduce the concentration and segregation
of commercial and different types of residential land use in
an effort to guide development according to the partially self-
sufficient neighborhood-unit concept. Part of the employed
population would work in tertiary activities and small industry within the neighborhood unit, while others working in
large-scale industry would commute to industrial zones. The
degree to which this pattern can be achieved is limited, of
course, because the major portion of the urban center is already built up.

Heavy industrial development is planned for the eastern
end of the city, downwind and downstream from dense population settlement. Green belts and forest parks are envisaged
as the "lungs of the city." The plan and development program
provide the basis for coordinated locational decisions with
respect to transportation, industrial development, a sewage
system, pollution and flood control, recreation, and housing.

The urban plan includes classification of major land-
use categories in seven out of the nine urban communes in
Zagreb (the central-city area). Table 6 shows the changes
in land proportions forecast by the Zagreb Institute for Urban
Planning.

## TABLE 6

### Projected Shifts in Land Use in Seven Urban Communes of Zagreb

| Category | Area in Square Kilometers 1964 | 1994 |
|---|---|---|
| Residential | 31. 09 | 52. 43 |
| Crafts, shops | 3. 09 | 8. 91 |
| Public services | 3. 18 | 10. 31 |
| Manufacturing | 3. 39 | 20. 86 |
| Agriculture | 168. 44 | 42. 40 |
| Recreation and parks | 90. 45 | 119. 12 |
| Water | 6. 45 | 4. 15 |
| River harbor | - | 2. 85 |
| Water-supply accumulation | 1. 64 | 9. 87 |
| Eroded and unusable land | 15. 56 | - |
| Flood protection | - | 7. 94 |
| Roads and parking space | 5. 96 | 27. 05 |
| Railway | 0. 6 | 1. 94 |
| Special uses | 9. 15 | 31. 27 |
| Total | 339. 1 | 339. 1 |

Urban planning and investment planning (economic and
social) are harmonized in Zagreb at the city level.  The contacts between the two planning agencies have been very good;
some officials feel they have better relationships than might
be the case if they were administratively integrated.  A con-
scientious effort has been made, in investment programs, by
the economic planning agency to respect the locational concepts of the long-range urban-development programs.  The
urban-development plan is basically concerned with patterns
of land use and location of facilities, while the rate and magnitude of investments in urban infrastructure fall within the
rubric of the economic and social plans.  The operating agencies, such as the water corporation, the school funds, and
the transport agencies, contribute plans and proposals to both
planning agencies.

## IMPLEMENTATION OF PLANNING CHOICES

Only the thirty-year urban plan is legally binding upon
public authorities and private persons in Zagreb.  The full
impact of the plans--particularly the positive aspects that call
for investments, construction, or other action--comes through
the whole complex of decisions relating to taxation, budgeting,
credit and capital investments by all the public authorities and
operating enterprises, and through nearly the entire range of
local legislation.  All agencies and public corporations of the
city and communal units are in fact engaged in plan implementation.  There are, however, several administrative mechanisms that heighten the potential for successful implementation
of the plans.

### Economic Plans

The economic and social plans of the city are composed
of forecasts and policies to be carried out by separate measures of the public authorities.  Plans are supplemented by local legislation passed with plan policies in mind, particularly
regulations dealing with credit and tax revenues, and assembly
approval of investments, fares, and charges.  These measures are enforceable against private parties and communal
authorities in the same manner as other prescriptions of law.
Prior to 1965, important economic regulations were explicitly
passed as "instruments" of annual plans.  This integration of
regulatory measures and plans has created coordinating links

between planning policies and economic development. (As
legal supervision of enterprises and public-service corporations rests with the communes in which they are headquartered
however, enforcement of some city regulations is indirect.)

There is no legal impediment to the local assemblies'
changing the plan during the time period for which it was
adopted. In practice, however, local governments tend to
adhere to their plans and to conform their measures and policies to its general aims. Activities related to the plans are
systematically followed by the staff of the planning agencies,
and the plans are continually under review. If extraordinary
circumstances require, the plans are reviewed by city and
communal assemblies on the basis of materials prepared for
them by the planning staffs.

The city and communal budgets are among the most important single mechanisms for implementing the plans, even
though those budgets cover only a small part of the total financial outlay called for by them. Annual plans have encompassed all economic transfers (in percentages) in the urban
area, including government budgets, capital investment by
enterprises, revenues and expenditures of urban services and
special funds, social security payments, and other transactions. Discussion of local-government budgets has been conducted simultaneously with discussion of annual plans, and budget decisions are closely correlated with the planning choices.

Preparation of plans has been in the political limelight
and subject to public discussion far more than the budget,
which is sometimes discussed in the popular assemblies
simply as an annex to the plan. Preparation of the budget begins in October, when the city and communal assemblies discuss reports prepared by the respective finance departments
concerning implementation of the current budget over the past
nine months. After deciding upon changes in the current budget, the assemblies discuss perspectives for the following
year and decide upon the main lines to be followed in preparing
the draft budget. The finance departments of the city and communes collaborate closely on the preparation of the budgets,
which they base on materials prepared by the economic planning agencies. The draft budgets are discussed by the respective councils for economic and financial affairs of the local
assemblies, and preparatory work on the budget is completed
in the city's Committee for Planning and Finance (which also

deals with the plan).  The budget is then voted by all chambers of the city assembly.  While the communes have independent budget-making powers, preparation of communal budgets is closely coordinated by city officials.  Thus, the budget-
making process serves not only to coordinate city expenditure
with the city plan but also to coordinate communal budgets with
the city plan.

The city budget includes only expenditures by the city
government and not expenditures by the independent institutions
and funds that are involved in urban services.  The city budget
controls these only in so far as the assembly extends grants
under contract with such institutions.  For example, in the
1964 budget for the City of Zagreb, out of a total expenditure
of slightly over 8 billion dinars, nearly 3 billion was grants,
of which about 1.78 billion dinars went to independent institutions, 790 million went to special funds, and 365 million
went to social organizations like hospitals and schools.  Grants
and direct investments together accounted for 65 per cent of
the city budget.  The relatively small proportion devoted to
operating functions reflects the degree of administrative decentralization, which was noted in connection with the small
number of city employees.  Thus, in spite of the integrated
planning and budgeting system in the city government, the
fragmented administrative pattern requires the cooperation of
many parties and agencies in plan implementation.

Implementation of the city budget itself is the primary
responsibility of the two types of administrative official:  the
chief administrative officer (the secretary of the city or commune, for example) and the chief accountant.  In no case are
the decision-maker and responsible accountant on any financial
transaction one and the same person.  The main structure of
the budget, that is the division among headings, can be changed
only by the assemblies.  Changes in more detailed items within
the budget categories can be made by executive and administrative organs.  Since 1965, lump-sum allocations to city
agencies are subdivided within the agency.

In summary, then, the plans of economic and social development are policy directives for all agencies and organs of
city and communal administration, both governmental and independent.  The power to implement plans through specific
investment is predominantly local, albeit scattered among two
tiers of local government and numerous separate agencies.

Only specific legal regulations are binding for enterprises,
funds, and public corporations; these are calculated to bring
about conformity with the plan in an indirect way.  Most direct implementing measures are contained in separate acts,
such as the budgets, and are enforced not by the planning
units but by the responsible substantive departments and
agencies of government.  As the special operating authorities
participate in the preparation of the plans, however, they
tend to cooperate in their implementation, and the political
organizations exercise influence on behalf of plan policies.

### Urban Plan

Particular arrangements utilized in Zagreb for land development and for control of land use and transfer have mitigated problems common to most urban areas of the world:
conflict and chaos in land-development programs and soaring
land values.

The thirty-year plan of urban development, as approved
by the city assembly and ratified by two thirds of the communes within the Zagreb urban area is, by contrast, directly
binding upon private parties and public authorities with the
force of law.  Prior to its adoption, implementation of the
plan and the general urban program was contingent upon the
voluntary cooperation of both city and commune authorities.
The respect paid to the plan prior to its adoption implies that
legal stature is not the essential determinant of plan impact in
Zagreb.  Independent agencies did not resist plan policies as a
rule; on the contrary, they complained that the failure of the
local governments to settle remaining controversies and to
adopt a permanent plan hampered their ability to establish and
carry out comprehensive development programs.

By law, the urban plan must be reviewed every five
years; actually, review tends to be continuous.

There are two major aspects to carrying out the urban
development program.  The first is active:  investment in and
construction of facilities envisioned in the program--South
Zagreb, new housing and community facilities, transport and
water supply extensions, etc.  The second is control of land
use, construction, and general physical development to ensure
locational conformance with the plan's design.

The first aspect engages the whole local-government process and all its administrative components and is, of course, subject to the omnipresent limitation of financial possibilities. Part of this type of implementation of the urban-development program is carried out through the city budget and economic plans. The economic plans within the urban area respect the urban program in designating the location of new industries and services. During each year's budgetary discussion, some elements of the urban-development program are taken up and financed, but at a pace that tends to lag behind expectations.

Within the framework of the existing urban program, the city assembly adopts a yearly program of land preparation and construction of utility lines and infrastructure. The Zagreb Institute for Urban Planning, the special authorities responsible for different local services, and the departments of building, housing, and communal affairs in both city and communes participate in preparing these land-development programs. The communal assemblies, neighborhood councils, and the general public are officially consulted before programs are submitted to the city assembly for decision. Site preparation for new projects established in these annual programs is financed by a special city fund, the Communal Utilities Fund of the City of Zagreb, an independent special fund established by the city in 1963 in order to undertake coordinated financing of local and public utility installations preparatory to development of new parts of the city and construction of public housing in them. Its jurisdiction is the entire urban area, and the fund is financed from indemnities paid by the user for the use of the land. The fund is managed by an independent board and a director, both appointed by the city assembly. It includes two major divisions--finances, and analysis and planning--and a number of smaller units, such as legal, technical, and general-administration offices.

A number of other special organs have been created by local government to finance implementation of the urban program. These have included the Zagreb Housing Fund (abolished in 1965) and the Development Agency for South Zagreb (incorporated into a new Institute of Communal Utilities in 1965). For the most part, construction necessary for implementing the urban program is undertaken by various independent corporations engaged in water supply, transportation, electricity and gas, construction, industry, and road

development.  These are consulted during preparation by the
city assembly of the annual land-development program; once
it is adopted, they must include their respective shares in the
projects in their own yearly work plans.  This method of organizing annual site preparation and construction does much to
avoid some of the problems of conflict or inadequate cooperation among operating agencies that are encountered in development projects in most urban areas of the world.

The second aspect of carrying out urban plans, land
control, is highly developed in Yugoslavia.  All land of an
urban character has been nationalized by federal law, under
which all buildings with more than two large or three small
flats and all building plots in "urban settlements" have been
transferred to public ownership, with compensation to their
former owners.  The extent of the territory included in an
"urban settlement" is determined by the city assembly, after
the Croatian Executive Council has decided generally which
areas in the republic are to be considered urban.  The Zagreb
Assembly has declared as "urban settlement" an area approximating seven of the nine urban communes of the city.  Persons can acquire the right to use this public land for building
purposes, in keeping with the urban plan, by participating in
public bidding which is organized by the commune.  The
former owners have priority rights to their former land for
building a house for their own use.  Public agencies and enterprises alike must compete for a use grant from the commune;
once this right of use is granted, it cannot be revoked as long
as the building put up by the user stands.

Land management and control is a specific function of
the constituent commune governments within Zagreb.  However, before a building permit can be issued by the responsible
department of the commune administration, the Zagreb Institute for Urban Planning must certify that the projected
building program conforms with the urban-development plan.
Buildings constructed without building permits or contrary to
the permit issued are liable, if they constitute a danger to
life or health, to be destroyed upon an administrative decision
taken by the commune's department of building, communal,
and housing affairs.  If there is no such danger, a building
without permit is subject to fine.  On-the-spot control is the
responsibility of the commune's building-inspection unit.

In addition to conformity to the general urban plan, conformity to building and land-use regulations is required for
issuance of a building permit.  These regulations are found
in a federal executive decree on building inspection, and, as
they specifically apply to the Zagreb urban area, in the
"Decision on the Preparation and Utilization of Land in the
Urban Area," passed by the city assembly in 1963.  No land
in the urban area can be used for building purposes before the
following conditions have been fulfilled:  1) preparation of the
land, including geological and technical surveys, draining,
leveling, and clearance; 2) construction of local infrastructure,
including roads, sidewalks, parking lots, lighting, recreation
facilities, water supply, gas, sewers, communication services, and transportation routes and stations.

In addition, minimum standards are controlled at the
point of issuing building permits.  Population densities and
other general standards of the urban plan are, however, not
directly controlled.

The complex building-permit procedure is thus an essential element in carrying out certain aspects of the urban plan
and enforcing urban construction requirements.  An application
for a building permit must be accompanied by a host of documents:  technical plans; approval by the urban-planning authorities; approval of the water-supply agency; approval of other
special organs, depending on the type of building; approval, in
the case of public buildings, of the local financial authorities;
and the contract with the commune under which the investor
has obtained the right to use the land.  The major drawback
to this somewhat cumbersome procedure is the time consumed:
usually three to six months.

In summary, land is allocated and managed, permits
issued, and inspection carried out by communal authorities;
regulation and approval in terms of plan goals are controlled
by city authorities.

Some major problems usually encountered in urban and
city planning, such as land speculation and scarcity of public
land, have been considerably reduced under the Yugoslav
system of urban landholding, particularly in Zagreb, where
the urban-area and urban-planning jurisdiction include land
subject to development for many years to come.  Nevertheless,
short-range economic factors as well as plan goals enter into

land-allocation decisions. The right to use a particular plot
is granted to the most favorable bidder. The amount of payment is considered the user's participation in expenditure to
develop the land. Government agencies must compete with
other parties in obtaining such grants, but in many cases
they can invoke priority of the public interest. In addition to
the fee for the grant, users of urban land pay continuing taxes
for the use of public facilities--such as roads, lighting, and
sewers--which are established by the communal assemblies
after consultation among all the communes in the "urban settlement" area. The tax varies with the size of building and
the zone in which the land is situated. The zones, especially
established for purposes of assessing the land-use tax, vary
with the quality of public facilities in the area. Outside the
area classified as urban settlement, in the rest of the city
and district, land in private ownership may be obtained by
government agencies through lengthier expropriation procedures.

## EVALUATION OF PLANNING
## IN THE ZAGREB AREA

Zagreb has tremendous advantages in planning in that
both physical and investment planning are organized on a
metropolitan scale, and the jurisdiction for such planning
coincides with that of a general urban government. Considerable undeveloped land for future construction falls within the
city limits. The fact that the local economic plans are components of a national system of planning allows both local and
higher government to be harmonized with respect to the urban
area. Yet local investment decisions can be made without
lengthy or complex approval procedures involving central
grants and authorities. Furthermore, there are within Zagreb several important arrangements for plan implementation,
particularly the annual land-development program, the close
relationship between economic planning and budgeting, and
the use of strong land controls.

The theoretical concepts and practical methods of economic and social development are newly evolving in Yugoslavia with the loosening of economic control. On the other
hand, there has been longer technical experience in urban
planning, and this has not been as directly affected by changes
as the socioeconomic framework of Yugoslav society. It is

therefore not surprising that the technical aspects of urban
planning in Zagreb have in general been judged more favorably
than those of social and economic planning.  In addition, the
urban plans are calculated for much longer time periods,
and the planners consequently have more time for careful
preparation.  The recent lapse of annual plans removes the
time pressure from investment planners but may weaken the
relationship between plans and budgets.

On the other hand, the work of various public service
institutes and agencies has been better coordinated with economic plans than with physical plans.  Agency work schedules
have been geared to the same time period as the investment
plans, which integrate public-service needs into the total investment picture for the metropolis.

In Zagreb, large numbers of people do participate in
discussing and commenting on draft plans.  This is a consequence of the essentially pluralistic character of plan preparation, plan approval, and plan implementation.

The hierarchical relationships among plans at different
government levels has been fairly well established; those plans
that are territorially more comprehensive are progressively
more general.  The plans in the communes are essentially the
coordinated sums of the plan proposals by individual enterprises and organizations within the framework of city financial
regulations.  City plans in turn are the coordinated sums of
commune-plan proposals with additional programs for city-
wide developments.  This type of planning system poses in-
tricate technical problems.  The methodology employed to resolve them is still not systematized, solutions are often im-
provised, and articulation of plans for different time periods
is still not satisfactory.

Local officials feel that the difficulties of economic
planning mount with the ratio of economic base to the size of
jurisdiction, because the impact of external forces on a small
unit, such as the city, rises with industrial expansion within
it.  Industries within metropolitan Zagreb have considerable
contacts and exchange with the suppliers, customers, and
labor market outside it.  They are influenced by technological
advances, ideas, and migration from without.  These factors
are in large part variables independent of influence from local
plans and have proved difficult for local planners to assess.

The larger the planning jurisdiction, the more the relevant factors are internal, and the more feasible it is for planners to apply statistical equalization procedures to prepare for unforeseen events.  For example, projections of tourism in a small resort may be thrown off by a spell of bad weather. In a larger territory, however, exceptionally good and bad weather conditions are more likely to offset each other.

This general proposition expresses the difficulties of decentralizing economic planning that are being experienced in Zagreb and throughout Yugoslavia.

Present-day planning and economic control in Zagreb consist  of a mixture of direct administrative controls (the postwar system) and indirect influences of plan targets and investment programs.  In theory, the Yugoslavs are reaching toward an economic system in which free initiatives of independent economic actors (special authorities, public corporations, and other working organizations) are only indirectly influenced by plans setting forth social and economic objectives.

Difficulties in plan implementation are, however, posed by the fragmentation of operating authorities at present.  Local officials are willing to continue to adjust the organizational framework in order to ease these difficulties.  At present, city authorities are discussing the possibility of reorganizing urban Zagreb as one commune. [3]

Several other proposals for improvement in planning are under discussion in Zagreb.  These include:

1.  To improve the technical aspects of planning (particularly economic and social planning) by introducing electronic data-processing equipment and elaborating systematic planning methodologies.  Safeguards, however, to protect the role of the public and representative assemblies in planning would be provided.

2.  To establish a university-level planning school to train economists and administrators for key technical planning roles.

3.  To amalgamate the city and commune agencies for urban planning.

4.  To create a committee for implementation of urban plans.  It would be composed of both planning technicians and political representatives.  Responsible to the city assembly, it would supervise and coordinate plan-implementation activities.


## NOTES TO CHAPTER 4


1.  The Statistical Institute of Zagreb was established by the city government and in 1965 absorbed by the Center for Economic Development, but the statistical service functions nationwide.  The local statistical units are linked by stronger bonds of administrative control than exist in other fields of activity.  Data are collected in censuses held every ten years, as well as by periodic and special surveys.  In addition, the Zagreb Planning Institute has periodically published analyses of financial reports of economic enterprises, comparative analyses of the city plan and the commune plans, reports on economic development by areas and branches of activity, and reports on demographic problems as they relate particularly to employment and productivity.

2.  The direct authority for their creation is a republic law on "urbanistic and regional land-use planning."  This law empowers the assemblies to organize either technical commissions for urban planning or, when the size of the task calls for it, more elaborate machinery, the institutes.

3.  These issues reinforce findings in other urban areas studied in this series that realistic decentralization of both planning and administration may consist of devolution not to the smallest possible units but to units on the scale found to correspond meaningfully to social and economic spheres of influence.

CHAPTER **5** SELECTED URBAN
SERVICES

Examination of four services in Zagreb illustrates
standard patterns of administration that are emerging across
a wide range of activity. Administrative arrangements for
water supply, mass transit, government housing programs,
and education were investigated with the aim of identifying the
types of public agencies involved in planning, financing, and
operating them, and the administrative problems and relationships encountered. In all four clusters of activity, we find
semi-autonomous local institutions providing the services
under the guidance of local government committees and executive councils and within the circumscriptions of federal and
republic regulation. Organizations with metropolitan-wide
jurisdiction play a role in all four, but a more important role
in water and transportation.

## WATER SUPPLY

The single operating agency in water supply is the Water
System of Zagreb, established in 1878 as a government agency
and transformed into a public corporation in 1947, by act of
the city government (then the People's Committee of the City
of Zagreb). Workers' management was established three years
later, when a workers' council elected by all employees was
instituted. (See Chart 3.)

The director of the Water System is selected by its
workers' council from candidates proposed by a special nominating committee. Half of this nominating committee is selected by the workers' council, and half by the assembly of
the commune in which the Water System is headquartered. [1]
(This is a typical example of the role of the communes in supervising enterprises located within their territory even
though the enterprise operates in a city-wide area.) By law,
the nominating committee must sponsor public competition
for the post, and candidates must fulfill specific professional

CHART 3

THE WATER SYSTEM CORPORATION OF ZAGREB
(1964)

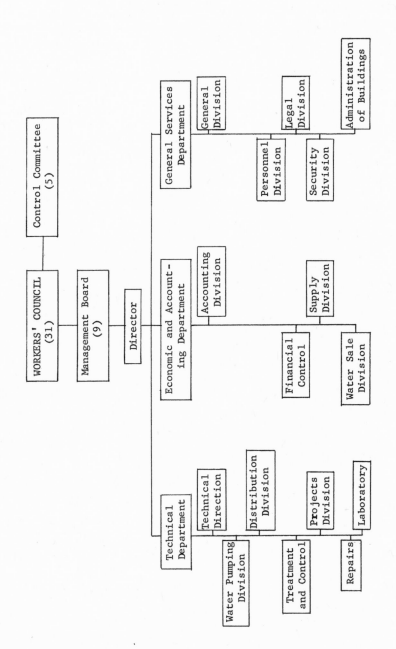

Note: Numbers in parentheses represent staff.

87

qualifications.  The professional director is elected for four
years and must turn to the workers' council for reappointment after that period.  On the basis of legally prescribed
competition, other leading officials of the Water System are
appointed by the workers' council, and lower officials are
appointed by the director.  These procedures are organized
by the personnel department of the corporation, but appointments can be made only if they are included in a job plan
previously approved by the workers' council.

The formal duties and responsibilities of the Water System, which has an independent legal personality and budget,
are set forth in its charter, which was adopted by its own
workers' council and approved by the Zagreb City Assembly.
They are:  building and maintenance of pumping stations and
reservoirs; building and maintenance of a distribution network; operation of all facilities for the supply of potable water
to users throughout the urban area; and manufacture, purchase,
and resale of water installations for dwelling units.  The system is the major supplier and distributor of water throughout
the urban area, but by recent arrangement the production and
sale of water meters (the principal product manufactured by
the Water System) has been transferred to another enterprise.

In 1961, the Water System supplied about 60 per cent of
the residential population of the urban area; the remainder--
primarily south of the railroad and on the outer fringes of
Zagreb--was outside the network of the public water-supply
system and provided for its needs from private wells and
springs.  About half of all industrial enterprises have their
own water-supply systems.  Industrial enterprises are required to apply to the Water System for prior authorization to
construct their own wells, but the Water System generally
does not enforce that provision and settles for a lump-sum payment by the enterprise for use of water resources.[2]  In addition to directly supplying the nine-commune urban area, the
Water System assists, on a contractual and commercial basis,
in constructing local water systems in satellite settlements in
other parts of the Zagreb District.

As a general economic enterprise, the Water System
comes under the rules of workers' management and has formal
relationships with the communal assembly, which supervises
the legality of its actions.  On the other hand, the Water System is designated as a public corporation because of the

essentially social nature of the service that it provides. This designation gives the Zagreb city assembly certain clearly defined powers in relation to it. The city assembly is responsible for policy supervision and cooperation. This role is fulfilled on a day-to-day basis by the councils and committees of the assembly and by the small staff in the city department of building, communal, and housing affairs. The Water System's immediate contacts with city government are with the two-man professional staff of the water-supply and sewer subunit of that department.[3]

The department of building, communal, and housing affairs is the most important general-government unit in the urban-service sector. Its internal organization is outlined in Chart 4. It has jurisdiction over the metropolitan area as a city agency, and has certain duties of district administration in the rural portions of the Zagreb District. The department head is appointed by the city assembly. Other employees in it, including staff of the water unit, were appointed by the city personnel commission until 1965. Since then, they have been appointed by the current employees of the department--usually acting through their council--in agreement with the director. Employees serve a probationary period of two years before becoming permanent. On questions of policy, the department head is responsible to the city assembly through its Council for Economic and Financial Affairs, and on questions of administrative procedure, to the secretary of the city.

The legal powers of the city government over the Water System are precisely defined. The assembly approves the price list for water services and approves interest rates to be paid on the working capital of the corporation. It approves the annual capital investment plans of the Water System and has participated in financing them. In practice, the assembly generally faces the alternative of approving higher prices for water services and letting the corporation finance a large part of its capital investments, or reducing prices and contributing to water investment out of general tax funds. The city controls the quality and sanitary standards of water distributed by the Water System on the basis of higher laws on health and sanitation standards. In addition, it approves the technical regulations on water use that are adopted by the workers' council of the Water System, and it must approve any changes in the content of the activity of the system or its integration with other organizations.

CHART 4

DEPARTMENT OF BUILDING, COMMUNAL, AND

HOUSING AFFAIRS OF THE CITY OF ZAGREB

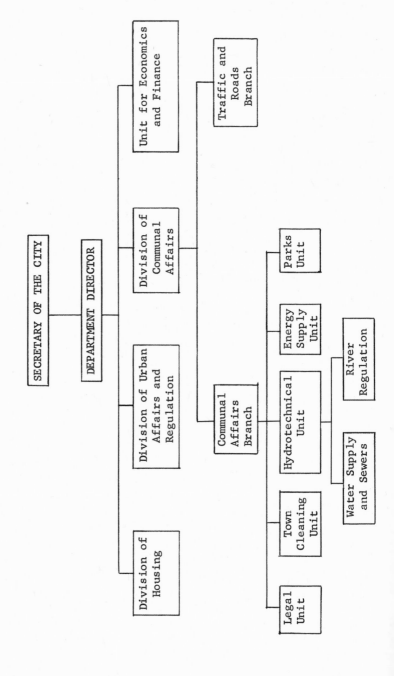

The major regulatory measures governing water supply
are a federal law on the protection of potable water, a Republic of Croatia law on the protection of water resources, and
a city decision regulating the watershed area of Zagreb.

## Water Finance

Operating expenditure relating to public water supply in
the urban area is entirely that of the Water System Corporation, with the exception of the salaries of the two professional
hydro-engineers in the water-supply and sewers unit, which
are paid out of the city budget. The general expenditure of
the Water System for 1963 was approximately 1.3 billion
dinars. The planned budget for 1964 amounted to 1.6 billion
dinars but, calculated on the basis of 1963 prices, the increase
was to only 1.5 billion dinars. This expenditure is financed
totally out of the operating revenues of the Water System,
which amounted in 1963 to 2.1 billion dinars, of which over
60 per cent were derived from the sale of water. The revenue
from all water users, including public agencies, is obtained
by metered charges, with minor exceptions. The rest of the
general revenue of the Water System is obtained from sale
of other goods and services, such as connecting main lines
with supply points, maintenance of water meters, repairs,
and sale of installations to enterprises and private households.
The planned revenue of the Water System for 1964 amounted
to about 3 billion dinars in 1963 prices, two thirds of which
was to come from the sale of water. The increase resulted
from a price rise approved by the city assembly with a view
to providing, at least partly, for extensive capital improvement planned for the next several years. [4]

The factors involved in the city assembly's decision on
water prices are both political and technical. It determines
whether the Water System is functioning efficiently and, therefore, if its forecast of operating expenditures is realistic and
acceptable. It can accept the assessment of operating costs
by the Water System, however, and still refuse to approve
the corresponding price list. In this case, the city assembly
must refund the Water System the difference between the revenue based on lower approved prices and the expenditure calculated by the system on actual operating costs and the legal
minimum salaries. In practice, prices covering operating
costs are approved, and the most frequent practical problem
is whether capital improvements by the Water System should

be financed from water prices or from city tax revenues.  In
the first case, water prices would be set high enough to provide revenue to cover not only the operating costs of the
Water System but also its capital investment.  In the second
case, the prices would be set to cover operating costs, while
capital investment would be derived from grants by the city
assembly.  Usually a compromise between these methods has
been adopted, depending on the judgment by the city assembly
as to the political impact of increases in the prices of water,
and on general price-wage policy prevailing at a given time
in the nation.

### Organizational Issues

The major problem in water-supply administration in
Zagreb has been the relationship of the corporation to general
government, particularly the local governments.  The central and Croatian governments have very minor roles with
respect to water supply in Zagreb.  They have issued binding
regulations dealing with sanitary standards of water and the
financial management of economic enterprises.  A certain
element of central control can be seen in the activities of the
inspection services, particularly the sanitary and financial
inspections, which, although they are local, have strong vertical ties to central services.  Other higher-government activities affect water supply in Zagreb only in an incidental and
indirect way, such as the involvement of the central government in the regulation of the Sava River flow, an important
source of water supply in the city.

The relationship of the water corporation to the commune of Medveščak, where its seat is located, and to the city
government is in issue.  The Water System comes under the
constitutional rule that legal supervision of enterprises is to
be by the commune only.  Although the commune's powers
over the corporation are limited, they can be used to gain
special advantages from the Water System.  Moreover, they
complicate the dealings of the city government with the corporation that services the entire urban area and not just the
commune where the corporation happens to be headquartered.
Responsibility for water-supply policy is vested by charter in
the city government.  As a result, both governments--city
and commune--maintain formal and informal relationships
with the corporation.  This entails some duplication of effort
and controversy.

A second problem, more complex, concerns the basic
question of the constitutional position of economic enterprises
that perform public services.  What do the principles of
autonomy and workers' self-management of enterprises imply
in terms of the delineation of responsibilities between corporation and local government in the case of a public-service
activity?  Some special provisions have been made by national
law for this type of activity.  The Basic Law on Water pro-
claims that water-supply activities are of public interest,
which allows city-assembly delegates to participate in the governing council of the Water System in Zagreb.

The City of Zagreb is, and local experts believe that it
should be, responsible for water-supply policy in the urban
area.  In spite of this fact, responsibility has increasingly
shifted to the Water System Corporation, with the city limiting
itself to exercising its formal approval powers.  As the corporation is financially self-supporting, its independence is
considerable.

The dominant factor in the growth of the corporation's
independence and power has been the effort by local authorities
to implement fully the constitutional system of functional decentralization, minimizing government interference in the independent working organizations.  Officers of the city government have leaned over backwards not to interfere, and have
tried to dismantle most of the administrative machinery within
the city government that might be guilty of such interference.
For this reason, the water and sewers unit was reduced to two
professionals.

A second factor contributing to the limited role of the
city government is the growing demand on scarce resources--
particularly of money and staff--which is rising so steeply that
any shift of burden to another agency is viewed with some re-
lief.  As a result, the city government's responsibility for the
water supply has become more formal than meaningful.  Work
on establishing a long-term plan for solving problems of water
supply in the urban area and for the larger region is lagging.
There is not even available a dependable detailed map of
existing water installations in the city.  At the same time,
among the groups concerned with water supply in the city, the
interests of the corporation itself are dominant.  It is unrealistic to expect that management bodies of the corporation

would be ready always and in all circumstances to give precedence to a rather hazy and ill-defined public interest over
and above the very tangible and concrete interests of the corporation itself and its employees.

The department of building, communal, and housing
affairs recently prepared a regulatory provision spelling out
more clearly the reciprocal rights and duties of the Water
System and the local government, but it was not passed by
the city assembly.  Current discussions may lead to a new
federal or republic law extending the power of government
authorities over local utilities.

### Appraisal

The Zagreb Water System operates with high depend-
ability to produce healthful potable water in a quantity that is
locally considered adequate for present needs of the population
served.  The Water System distributed an average of 96, 712
cubic meters per day in 1963, [5] an increase of about 38 per
cent over the 1950 output.  Less than 2 per cent of the total
water distributed is through common public outlets.  The approximate average per capita daily consumption within the
service area was .28 cubic meters.  The 1964 prices for
water were such that at existing consumption levels, an average four-person household spent about 1,344 dinars per month
on water, or about 3 per cent of the average salary of employed persons. [6]

On the other hand, the fact that a portion of the urban-
area population is not served by the system is considered
undesirable.  Moreover, official estimates of 1970 needs,
based on stable consumption levels but increasing population
and expanded coverage of the system, call for an increase of
34 per cent over 1964 distribution.  This would require nearly
doubling the annual rate of capacity increase of the past decade
This expansion is called for generally in the various plans for
Zagreb.

### Planning for Water-Supply Expansion

A water-supply improvement plan for Zagreb has been
developed over a long period since the first surveys were conducted in 1932.  Current problems are with completing it and
integrating it into the general long-range urban plan and into

short-range economic plans and investment programs through
which it can be carried out.

As technical expertise on water-supply problems is
concentrated in the Water System Corporation, its staff is
the major source of plan proposals.  On the other hand, primary planning responsibility rests with the Zagreb Institute
for Urban Planning and the Zagreb Center for Economic Development.  Difficulties have been encountered in delineating
the respective roles of the operating agency and the planning
institutes.  The department of building, communal, and
housing affairs serves as a contact and clearinghouse between
them.

Once plans are completed and approved by the city
authorities, the water corporation has full responsibility for
fulfilling them.  (The approved long-range urban plan is
binding upon it.)  The corporation undertakes the capital construction itself or through contracts with construction enterprises.  According to present policies of the city government,
the Water System itself will provide most of the investment
capital required for plan implementation in the future.  The
long-range urban plan (1963-93) assumes an increase in population of the urban area to 975,000 by 1993 and an increase in
the percentage served by the Water System to 90 per cent.
Daily average capacity of the system should be increased,
according to the plan, to 288,000 cubic meters by adding four
new pumping zones and expanding the distribution networks to
the south, west, and east.  This plan has not been spelled out
in monetary terms.

The draft seven-year development plan for the urban
area proposed that the system be extended to 77 per cent of
the population by 1970.  On the basis of its assumption of a
total population increase to 572,000, water supply must be
expanded to serve 167,400 more users.  This was to be achieved
by constructing new pumping stations (in the zone delineated
in the urban plan) and ten new reservoirs, as well as increasing the capacity of existing facilities.  The total capital
requirements foreseen by the plan were 7 billion dinars.

Progress has been lagging in terms of these targets.
After two years of public discussions, Zagreb's seven-year
development plan was actually adopted as a five-year plan.
The major obstacles, however, to timely investment in water-

supply improvements in past years have been financial. This
is demonstrated by the case history of one large-scale water
project--a new collection, purification, and distribution system at Mala Mlaka on the southern bank of the Sava River.
The first phase of this project--including three reservoirs
with pumping stations and a main line to the city--was completed in 1964 at a total cost of 2.6 billion dinars. As the
policy of the city assembly prior to that time had been not to
burden the price of water with capital costs, most of the funds
were derived from tax revenues--grants from general budgets
and loans from the housing and communal utilities funds.

The first surveys for this project were undertaken in
1932; an initial work program established in 1936 was inter-
rupted by the war. After the war, the city authorities were
unwilling to commit the necessary funds for the project. Its
major proponents were the professional staff in the hydrotechnical unit of the city administration, who kept pointing out
the importance of a long-term solution to water-supply problems. They were represented to the public through the press,
and they propounded their technical arguments in discussions
with city planners, engineers, and economists. Effective opposition was generated by the competition among a large number of urban-development projects for available resources.
The first turning point came in 1951, when the city assembly
decided to proceed with construction of a new part of the city
on the south bank of the river. This provided an immediate
incentive to allocate funds to waterworks in the Mala Mlaka
area, which is in the vicinity of South Zagreb. In addition, a
succession of summer droughts, during which water consumption had to be limited, dramatically demonstrated existing deficiencies. In 1953, on the initiative of the city hydrotechnical
unit, the influential Council for Communal Affairs (one of the
sixteen executive councils of the city assembly, which was
abolished when the councils were reorganized in 1964) persuaded the assembly to commit funds to the first phase of the
Mala Mlaka project.

The flow of funds remained inadequate, however, and
there was little hope of obtaining a greater share of the much-
claimed city investment fund for water. As the Water System
Corporation grew more independent, it was in an increasingly
unfavorable position to compete for city resources. This

situation finally led to a decision by the assembly that a significant portion, and later the bulk, of necessary investments
be supplied from user charges.  There followed a steady increase in prices.

This history of fiscal decisions is demonstrated in the
growth rate of investment in the project, which is shown
Table 7.   The sudden jumps in 1957 and 1963 reflect
price rises.

This policy provided a solution to the financial problem
that was likely to lead, under normal circumstances, to political opposition by the users.  There was, however, no significant opposition, primarily because of existing inflationary
trends and a steady rise in all prices as well as in nominal
wages.  All public utilities, local transportation, rents, and
local taxes shared in the increase.  The somewhat steeper
increase in the price of water was felt less because water was
the least expensive public utility.  Moreover, the Water System
Corporation has tried to soften potential opposition to price
increases by public-relations campaigns explaining the necessity and usefulness of capital improvements to be financed by
its revenues.

Decision-making for plan implementation with respect to
water will thus be fairly concentrated in the future, as the
Water System will be providing the bulk of investment necessary as long as the city assembly retains its present policy.
The major administrative problem will be to stabilize and improve the comparatively new arrangement by which the responsibility for programming, construction, and operation is
delegated to the autonomous corporation.  Some experts feel
that delegation of powers has proceeded too far and that the
city assembly should retain greater authority in order to be
able to conduct long-term supply policy.  They would seek a
balance between the operational responsibilities of the Water
System and the planning and policy-making responsibilities of
city government.  City officials, on the other hand, consider it
impossible to exempt the Water Systems from the prevailing
principles of functional decentralization under the federal
Constitution, which guarantees to working enterprises and
institutions a meaningful degree of autonomy.

## TABLE 7

Authorized Expenditure on Mala Mlaka
Water-Supply Project*

| Year | Investments (1,000 dinars) |
|------|---------------------------|
| 1950 | 9,869 |
| 1951 | 2,341 |
| 1952 | 46,457 |
| 1953 | 114,750 |
| 1954 | 125,359 |
| 1955 | 142,740 |
| 1956 | 102,494 |
| 1957 | 512,222 |
| 1958 | 488,000 |
| 1959 | 443,318 |
| 1960 | 413,179 |
| 1961 | 484,696 |
| 1962 | 624,505 |
| 1963 | 1,885,279 |

* Source: Vodovod grada zagreba 1878-1963 (Zagreb: 1964), p. 112.

Finally, one might speculate whether the ambitions for water-supply expansion included in the long-range urban plan for Zagreb can be financed out of current water revenue alone without putting a tremendous burden on the water price in future years.

## PUBLIC HOUSING

Since 1958, management of dwelling units in urban portions of Yugoslavia has been standardized under the "Law on the Nationalization of Urban Land and Dwelling Houses. " A unique system of urban land and housing management underlies and influences the characteristics of government housing programs in Zagreb. A second major factor in housing-program administration is the policy of decentralization, both functional and territorial, resulting in frequent changes in organization, which first shifted functions from higher government to the city and communes, and then shifted them from general local-government units to special semi-autonomous institutions in the urban area.

Throughout these developments, government attention to housing problems has been gradually growing. Although housing has been the category of the most severe problems in Zagreb since the war, investment priorities understandably were given to productive enterprise, at first to achieve economic reconstruction and currently to sustain economic development. The problem of housing is nonetheless acute in Zagreb and is one of the most discussed topics in voters' meetings, the press, and political organizations. Over half of the buildings in the urban area are substandard by local measures, [7] chiefly because of overcrowding. Official estimates hold that 40, 000 additional dwelling units are currently required to accommodate new household formation in the urban area (35, 000 of these are needed in the central-city area), and 35, 000 to replace substandard dwellings (30, 000 of these are needed in the central-city area). An additional 10, 000 would be necessary to house population increases to 1975.

The scope of Zagreb's housing problems is attributable to the rapid population growth resulting from migration. The Yugoslav Constitution guarantees the right of free movement, preventing city and district authorities from legislative and administrative restrictions on migration. The policies of

Croatian and Zagreb authorities designed to control the demand for housing have concentrated on two objectives: 1) to improve regional communications with the ultimate aim of integrating the towns of Sisak and Karlovac (both over thirty miles from Zagreb) into the Zagreb metropolitan region and building residential colonies along transportation lines (see Frontispiece Map); and 2) to provide urban facilities in the rural area around Zagreb in order to stem the flow from village to town.

As mentioned in Chapter 4, most of the land in the Zagreb urban complex is publicly owned and is managed and allocated by the communal governments. No matter who builds, all houses with three or more flats are managed in a manner prescribed by federal law.

Until 1965, each building was managed by a house council elected for one year by all adults living in the building. Thus, major residential buildings were social-management organizations. The council employed a superintendent and collected rents.

The establishment and disposal of rental income was standardized by law. Through 1965, rents for new dwellings were calculated on the basis of a depreciation time span of 100 years. The present value of the dwelling, which takes into consideration building costs and interest, was divided into 1,200 parts (100 years times 12 months) to obtain half the monthly rent. This figure was doubled to arrive at the total monthly rent. Half the rental income was left with the house council for maintenance, small repairs, and expenditures incidental to administration of the house. The other half, the "depreciation fund," was pooled by the city government and divided between city and commune housing-construction funds. Thus, current rentals were used to finance new construction. For old houses, the method of calculation was the same, with the original building price spread over 100 years and the depreciated present value taken as the basis for assessing rent. This system limited the rent to levels that were unrealistic from the point of view of replenishing the housing funds, but that were adapted to the general level of incomes in the country. One hundred years is a very long depreciation span (compare this with loans for housing construction, which must be repaid within thirty years), and rising prices transformed the rent-calculation procedure for all practical purposes into a rent ceiling.

In 1965, a new federal law on public housing altered
this system.  Greater latitude is allowed for calculation of
rents.  More important, and still controversial, the law calls
for establishing neighborhood, communal, or city enterprises
to collect rents, maintain buildings, and become major investors in new housing within their jurisdictions.  These
would, therefore, assume the functions of both individual
house councils and local housing-construction funds.

Rents are expected to rise to adequate levels to make
new building and sale and rental of dwellings to individuals
and organizations economically feasible for the housing enterprises.

Since passage of this law, the housing-construction funds
in Zagreb have been abolished.  The new enterprises are
organizing slowly, but the whole concept is being challenged
in the constitutional courts as contrary to the constitutional
principle of self-management of residential buildings by their
inhabitants.

There is practically no private building for the market
in Zagreb.  Private construction is limited to family houses of
one or two flats, and there are a number of private building
craftsmen, employing up to five men, who operate this sector.
For the most part, however, investors in housing construction
in the Zagreb urban area have been either cooperatives and
economic enterprises building for the use of their own members or government housing-construction funds.  Cooperatives
and enterprises receive subsidies from public agencies in the
form of site preparation, credit under favorable conditions,
and construction of public facilities and utilities.  This study
concentrated on the activities undertaken directly by the public housing agencies, particularly the Zagreb City Fund for
Housing Construction and the commune funds for housing construction.

After the initial postwar period of reconstruction, housing in Yugoslavia generally, and in Zagreb in particular, lagged
behind industrial development.  During the period of government centralization, housing construction was handled chiefly
as an adjunct to building new factories, with a sum for employee housing included in the centrally determined plans for
industrial development.  Later, as the growing housing shortage received increasing attention and government policy shifted

to gradual decentralization, local authorities came to play a
more and more important role in housing. At present, the
role of the federal and republic governments has for the most
part been restricted to regulation. The basic legal texts in
the housing field have been the federal laws of 1959 on financing
housing construction and on housing management, together
with the 1965 legislation on rents and housing enterprises. At
present, if the federal or republic authorities want to build
housing in the urban area (for example, housing for their civil
servants), they are in the same position as any other investor,
and may build by direct arrangement with a construction enterprise or seek the cooperation of a housing enterprise. Beyond
this, there has been no direct participation by federal and
republic authorities in housing-construction programs in the
Zagreb area.

In keeping with the concepts of functional decentralization
of power throughout the fabric of society, the role of general
government as a whole in housing has been reduced. The
housing departments of the communes were responsible for
allocating dwellings as well as land at one point, but this
proved impracticable and fell into disuse even before it was
formally abrogated. In the late 1950's and early 1960's, Yugoslav administrative experts and political leaders were concerned with avoiding cumbersome bureaucratic machinery in
housing. Thus, in Zagreb, in order to relieve the city administration, as well as the administrative machinery of the communes, of the huge task of implementing housing programs,
special housing-construction funds were created. At the same
time, the prevailing policy was to gradually shift the financial
burden for housing construction from public budgets and public
funds to the resources of individuals (in cooperatives) and organizations. Less of the national income, generally speaking,
should be channeled through public budgets and more of it distributed through individual income; but individuals and their
associations should then be responsible for paying the greater
share of the costs of what they utilize. This policy was bolstered by the negative aspects of too much administrative interference in the allocation and distribution of dwellings. Thus,
the present pattern of organization for public-housing activities
is new and rapidly changing due to the effort to implement these
general policies.

## The Housing Agencies

Through 1965, the major public agency involved in housing in Zagreb was the City Fund for Housing Construction, an independent public fund organized by the city government to operate throughout the urban area. It was run by a management board and director, both of whom were appointed by the city assembly. While independent in its day-to-day operations, the fund was politically responsible to the city assembly, which approved its annual investment programs. It financed and managed housing on its own account. It also managed construction projects to which various enterprises and public agencies contributed capital; in such cases, it was a conduit for investment in dwelling construction by other parties. Third, it loaned capital to other investors, either by participating in costs of projects that it managed for them or by loaning to enterprises and cooperatives that built for themselves.

The housing construction funds of the constituent communes in Zagreb were organized by the communal assemblies along similar lines and had powers and responsibilities analogous to those of the city fund. The division of functions between city and communal funds was according to the size and complexity of tasks. Communal funds financed repair and rehabilitation work and aided private construction; the city fund aided major construction by enterprises and cooperatives and undertook large-scale housing developments. The important power held by the city in this relationship was its authority to divide the revenue from the depreciation fund (half of all rents paid in the city) between city and communal housing-construction funds. Under the new system, independent housing enterprises will control rental revenues, thereby further reducing control by general government.

The Institute of Communal Utilities, established in 1965 and incorporating the former Development Agency for South Zagreb, is another special authority involved in residential development. Begun as a special-development authority for turning a rural section of the area into an integral part of the modern metropolis, it has been given more general jurisdiction and responsibility. The city assembly approves its work programs.

The Development Agency for South Zagreb had been responsible for implementing work on that project and coordinating other public agencies as they operate in the area. It participated with the Zagreb Institute for Urban Planning in designing South Zagreb, and was responsible for the detailed programming of construction work and determination of priorities. It was authorized to purchase agricultural land and buildings, to assume the normally communal responsibility for management of nationalized land within that area, to undertake land surveys, to organize work on site preparation and construction of public infrastructure, and to coordinate public investors operating there (these have included the housing funds, enterprises, and the Communal Utilities Fund). Communal authorities consult the agency in granting building permits within South Zagreb.

The Communal Utilities Fund, another independent public fund, was created by the city in 1963 to provide coordinated financing of local facilities and public-utility installations preparatory to development of new parts of the city and construction of public housing in them.

The housing division of the department of building, communal, and housing affairs is the mother organization of these new independent agencies, which, although they have outstripped it in size, tend to regard the division as their central rallying point. Under the city charter, the department has responsibility only to enforce housing laws and regulations, to prepare draft acts for the city assembly, to implement decisions of the city assembly, and finally to exercise general supervision in the field. Although the housing division had shrunk to eleven employees by 1965, its operational role is greater and its enforcement role smaller than the charter provisions imply. It has been involved in the day-to-day coordination of the various housing agencies; enforcement of building and housing regulations is exercised by the building-inspection service, in a separate department. (See Chart 2.) The housing division is still the dominant source of housing policy, although the city housing fund, with eighty employees, was assuming that position before its abolishment. The new housing-management enterprises, if they work out, may further fragment power over housing.

Each communal administration has a housing unit of its own that performs similar functions and also finances community facilities (this is done on the metropolitan level by the Communal Utilities Fund).

Actual construction work for all types of residential building in the urban area is done by economic enterprises in the building business, operating under contract formerly with the housing-construction funds or with enterprises and cooperatives that are investing in housing.

## Finance of Public Housing

Apart from direct investment by enterprises and cooperatives in residential construction for use by their members and employees, the bulk of investment in housing has been by housing-construction funds. In the future, it is to be through the housing-management enterprises, using rental revenues and bank loans.

The sources of revenue of city and communal housing funds were the depreciation fund derived from all rentals in the city, an earmarked 4 per cent city tax on payrolls, income from sales and from interest on fund loans and deposits, and subsidies from the general local budgets. [8] The subsidies covered administrative costs of the funds.

The following figures are a breakdown of the revenues of the housing funds in 1963 (millions of dinars).

|  | Income from sales | Housing payroll tax | Local-government subsidy | Depreciation fund from rentals, plus interest income and enterprise contributions |
|---|---|---|---|---|
| City Fund | 3,466 | 5,105 | 71 | 5,368 |
| Communal Funds | 499 | 227 | 25 | 1,810 |

Thus, rents and earmarked housing tax revenues were channeled through the housing-construction fund for use in construction and repair. The new system will shift the burden to rents and bank loans.

Loans by the funds were granted in principle to the highest bidder, but in practice tended to be directed to the most pressing technical and social needs--for example, repair of badly dilapidated buildings and providing housing for people displaced by slum clearance.

The Communal Utilities Fund is financed from indemnities paid to the city for the use of public land--the land-use tax. The total revenues of the Communal Utilities Fund and Development Agency for South Zagreb were 55 million and 96 million dinars, respectively, in 1963.

The policy of shifting the burden of housing finance emerged in two steps. The city assembly had been reducing the subsidies from general taxes to the housing funds before the national law of 1965 called for their replacement by self-financing housing enterprises. The desire to shift the financial burden for housing investment to the user naturally links the progress of construction to the magnitude and expenditure patterns of personal incomes. As the figures for 1963 show, the income from sales and rents was far from adequate to cover housing-fund activities. Controversy over housing finance has been lively in Yugoslavia generally and in Zagreb in particular. The planners and housing bureaucracies have pressed for rent increases and a more realistic economic price policy in housing. [9]

In voters' meetings, political organizations, and local assemblies, the public has expressed vigorous opposition to substantial rent increases. The success of the new housing enterprises in maintaining planned rates of construction on a self-financing basis will rest on their ability to overcome this opposition.

### Planning and Rates of Investment

The housing-construction funds, particularly that of the city, and the housing division have cooperated with the Zagreb Institute for Urban Planning in drafting housing plans for Zagreb. The general planning agencies are responsible for coordinating public-housing programs with other aspects of urban development and including them in the comprehensive plans for adoption by city and communal political bodies. The long-term urban-development plan for Zagreb is supposed to establish the framework and targets for housing plans. Before

it was adopted, long-term housing planning proceeded by
continuing consultation between housing agencies and the Zagreb Institute for Urban Planning.

The presently agreed-upon long-term targets require an
increasing rate of construction, in five-year spans, as follows:

| Five-Year Span | New Dwelling Units per Year | Total |
|---|---|---|
| 1963-67 | 5,000-5,800 | 28,000 |
| 1968-72 | 5,800-7,000 | 33,000 |
| 1973-77 | 7,000-8,500 | 40,000 |
| 1978-82 | 8,500-10,300 | 48,000 |
| 1983-87 | 10,300-12,800 | 58,000 |
| 1988-92 | 12,800-16,000 | 74,000 |
|  |  | 281,000 |

The medium-range plans and yearly programs of housing
construction have been incorporated into seven-year and annual social and economic development plans for Zagreb, respectively. Thus, the housing programs have formed part of
the plan documents prepared by the city and communal planning institutes, and are in this way adopted by the respective
assemblies. The most recent proposal for expanding the housing program was a medium-range housing plan sponsored
jointly by the housing construction funds, the city and communal
housing divisions, the Zagreb Institute for Urban Planning, and
the Zagreb Planning Institute (now the Center for Economic
Development). The city housing division played the leading role
in its development. It was discussed and approved by the Council for Housing Affairs (one of the executive councils of the city
assembly that existed prior to the reorganization of the councils in 1964) and by the assembly's standing Committee for Planning and Finance. It was included in the Plan of Economic and
Social Development (1966-70) for Zagreb.

This housing plan called for building 53,000 new dwelling
units by 1970, of which 43,000 were to be built by the housing
funds (including units built exclusively with their own funds and

units built under cooperative arrangements for joint investment with enterprises and organizations).  This task will now
fall to independent enterprises and cooperatives.  The building
effort is to be concentrated in a few new residential areas,
particularly in South Zagreb.  The total expenditure forecast
for fulfilling this construction program is approximately 200
billion dinars at 1964 money values.

Once a year, the Zagreb Housing Construction Fund submitted to the city an annual housing-construction program,
which was integrated by the Zagreb Planning Institute into the
annual economic and social plan.  The annual program was
supposed to implement the seven-year plan.  This procedure
gave the planning institute an influential role in the investment
policy of the housing-construction fund.  It also assured that,
in approving the housing-investment program, the assembly
would consider related aspects of urban development and finance.  With the elimination of the fund and of detailed annual
city plans, voluntary cooperation among agencies will become
a more important device for coordinated development.

As the housing plans apply to both governmental and nongovernmental investment, implementation of them is contingent
upon the decisions of various enterprises and cooperatives.
The only role played by the Zagreb Institute for Urban Planning
in enforcing the housing plans is to consider them in approving
building-permit applications.

The goal of the medium-range plan--construction of
53,000 new dwelling units at a cost of some 200 billion dinars
by 1970--is not overambitious in terms of the needs estimated
by the city housing division, on the basis of data supplied by
the Institute for Urban Planning (85,000 dwelling units by 1975).
It is ambitious, however, in comparison with past investment
and construction rates.  The number of aided dwelling units
constructed from 1959 to 1964 in the Zagreb urban area totaled
23,553, as follows:

| | Constructed by Government or to Government Account | | Constructed with Government Aid | |
|---|---|---|---|---|
| | Urban Area | Central City | Urban Area | Central City |
| Public Housing Units for Sale at or Above Cost | - | - | 9,490 | 8,916 |
| Public Housing Units for Rent | 8,438 | 8,396 | - | - |
| Cooperative Housing Units for Sale at or Above Cost | - | - | 5,625 | 5,597 |

Total planned investment in housing by all public agencies, housing cooperatives, and economic enterprises building with public subsidies of any kind, amounted to 26 billion dinars in 1964. It had been rising rapidly. If we adjust the figure to correct for inflation, 1964 planned investment in housing was 18.5 billion dinars compared with 15.6 billion in 1963, 7.5 billion in 1960, and 5.5 billion in 1959, all in 1959 dinars. The degree to which local-government attention to housing problems has been growing is reflected in this real increase in planned investment of 233 per cent from 1959 to 1964.

## Problems of Housing Construction

The major obstacles to increases in investment and improvement in housing in Zagreb are not organizational, but financial and technical. These are limited financial resources, limited capacity of the building industry, scarcity of building materials, and scarcity of highly skilled specialists in the building trades. There are no serious complaints about lack of coordination in housing programs in the urban area, although the new system may pose some problems in this respect. Yugoslav reformers have been more concerned with eliminating cumbersome centralized bureaucratic machinery in housing than with having too many small agencies. Local housing-construction funds were considered an overconcentration of power. Critics of the new system, however, wonder whether excessive fragmentation might again turn the cost curve upward.

Because the problems of housing construction in Zagreb are primarily economic and technical, major attention has been directed to finding technical breakthroughs that might produce faster and cheaper construction. "From building craft to construction industry" has become the slogan of housing interests. Past experience with some innovations, bolstered by bureaucratic conservatism, however, has produced some skepticism in Zagreb of proposals as they are generated. Many ideas for improving housing construction have originated not with the housing authorities but with the construction enterprises in the urban area. A dramatic example is a method of prefabricated construction, the JU-61, developed and put on the market by Jugomont Corporation. The system uses standard, prefabricated elements that can be assembled in different ways to form several building types. Unlike existing systems of prefabricated building, JU-61 standard parts include final installation and craft work, which account for much of the time it takes to complete a house by traditional methods.

Immediately after the design was proposed, two camps developed in housing circles. Urban planners and housing technicians of the city administration were doubtful; other local experts, particularly the economists, were immediately in favor. The question was much discussed in the management board of the City Housing Construction Fund, the Council for Housing of the city assembly, and in the city assembly itself. In the meantime, Jugomont decided to put its system to the test. It persuaded a number of economic enterprises to use the design and organized a public technical review of the results, which received considerable publicity. The city assembly was convinced, and thereafter Jugomont obtained a large contract from the housing fund. Thus, the pressure exerted by a single influential enterprise was sufficient to overcome the opposition of the city technicians. The JU-61 has since stood the test of time; it is now utilized in other parts of Yugoslavia and has received international attention.


## MASS PASSENGER TRANSPORTATION

Urban transportation in Zagreb is organized in much the same way as water services. Transit services are provided by the Zagreb Electrical Tramway Corporation, which is an economic enterprise subject to the general rules of workers'

management.  However, it is further categorized as a public
service, giving the city government special responsibilities
toward it.

The Zagreb Electrical Tramway Corporation operates
all public tram and bus services in the urban area.  Its system consists of tram lines and two cable car lines within the
seven central communes; and a bus service network throughout the nine-commune urban area and extending, on a few
routes, into other parts of the Zagreb District.  Additionally,
the City Railway, a separate public corporation, operates one
narrow track railway between central Zagreb and a major
recreation area in the district.  The national railroad system,
of which Zagreb is a northern hub, provides some commuter
service in the district on its through trains.  At the same time,
about 500 taxicabs in the urban area are operated by several
independent enterprises and private owners; and bus services
are provided by large enterprises for their own employees.
Beyond these, the role of the private automobile in intra-urban
transport is just beginning to grow swiftly.  The number of
private automobiles registered in the Zagreb urban area
jumped from 14,000 in 1963 to 30,000 in 1965.

Traffic statistics indicate that the tramway company's
services dominate the urban transportation picture:

### Person Trips per Average Working Day

### Zagreb Urban Area, 1963

| | | |
|---|---|---:|
| 1. | Trams (Zagreb Electrical Tramway) | 503,000 |
| 2. | Public Buses (Zagreb Electrical Tramway) | 106,500 |
| 3. | Enterprise Buses | 5,500 |
| 4. | City Railway | 420 |
| 5. | Taxi | 7,350 |
| 6. | Private Motor Vehicle | 33,000 |
| | Total: | 655,770 |

In addition, on an average day about 14,000 persons leave Zagreb by train; some of these are intra-urban commuters, but railroad data does not give a breakdown of these figures.

Construction and maintenance of streets and roads in Zagreb is undertaken by another independent enterprise and various construction companies under contracts to commune and city governments. They are paid from special city and communal road funds that are derived from earmarked tax sources.

In addition to these operating agencies, various government units are involved in urban transportation. Aside from the railroad system, the role of central and republic government is limited to general regulation of the following subjects:

1. The organization and functioning of economic enterprises generally (including the transportation agencies in Zagreb).

2. The financial procedures of operating enterprises and agencies (for example, the provision that organizations of the "public corporation" type are to have their price lists approved by local-government authorities).

3. Standards of safety and quality for public transport services, and major traffic regulations.

The traffic and roads branch of the city department of building, housing, and communal affairs (see Chart 4) carries out the city assembly's duties, as outlined in the city charter, to supervise the transit corporations and to develop comprehensive transportation policies. The two city planning agencies have a major role in transportation planning, and the department of internal affairs, through its special police units, is responsible for control of road traffic safety. The commune in which the transit company is headquartered exercises the standard formal controls of a commune over enterprises.

Finally, the roster of actors in urban transportation for Zagreb includes several nongovernmental organizations--the Association for Technical Education, the Society of Motorists,

and the Association of Transport Engineers and Technicians--
that engage in technical training and express various interests
in relation to transportation developments.

### The Zagreb Electrical Tramway Corporation

The transit company, like all other economic enterprises falling under the general rules of workers' management, is run by a workers' council elected by all its employees, and by a management board elected by the workers' council each year.  The director of the company is appointed by
the council on recommendation of a nominating committee that
includes representatives of both the communal assembly and
the workers' council.  Although personnel administration is
conducted by the company's personnel department, ultimate
responsibility for personnel decisions rests with the workers'
council.  This arrangement supports a tendency to recruit
executives in the transit enterprise, as in other enterprises,
among the employees, in which case in-service training and
additional formal education is provided to qualify nonprofessional employees for professional posts.

The Zagreb Electrical Tramways Corporation includes
six departments, each of which has its own director and employee council.  These include: tramway transportation, responsible for the rolling stock of trams and cable cars as well
as minor repair services; buses, responsible for the rolling
stock, garages, and minor repair services; tramway workshops; bus workshops; construction; and administration.

The operating expenditure of the tramway company is
fully financed from fare revenues.  In 1963, total general expenditure by the company was 4,336 million dinars, while
total revenue from fares was 5,332 million dinars.  Outlay
from the city budget for public transportation that year, only
36 million dinars, was expended on modernizing traffic sig-
nals and installing traffic safety devices.  The fare structure
is based on a division of the area into four zones--the central
city and three others--each having the same basic fare for
internal trips.  In an interzone trip, an additional fare is
charged for each zone that is crossed.  As of September 1,
1964, the basic fare for both tramways and buses was 30
dinars.  Commercial rebates of one third are offered with the
purchase of fifty tickets, and special rebates of two thirds are
available to students, veterans, and certain other groups.

The relationship between the Zagreb Electrical Tramway
Corporation and the city government has been flexible over
the years.  The city has greater influence over urban transportation than its formal modes of control over the enterprise
would imply.  Although the full degree of autonomy contem-
plated by Yugoslav concepts of functional decentralization has
not yet been reached, the power and independence of the transit
enterprise have been increasing, particularly with its establishment as an autonomous working organization.

The corporation is entitled to plan its own activity, to
manage public property assigned to it (i. e. , its assets), to
hire employees, and to determine working conditions and the
distribution of its income.  (Surplus income can be distributed
to employees by the workers' council. )  At the same time, the
city assembly must approve the transit fares, which the city
can reduce below costs if it compensates the company accordingly.  The company is also obligated to coordinate its work
schedules with other city requirements, to notify local authorities of service interruptions, and to consult the public on decisions affecting its interests.  The workers' council must
discuss all proposals put forth by local voters' meetings or
the city assembly and notify these of the decisions taken.

While the relationship of the company with government
agencies is formally regulated by those legal provisions, the
informal limitations on its power are significant.  Operating
coordination of transportation matters is undertaken by the
transport and roads branch, although this section has been reduced to a staff of four (a secretary, two persons in the transport unit, one in the road unit), plus the branch chief.  The
branch is formally charged with analyzing the urban-
transportation situation and preparing decisions for the city
assembly and its councils.  The assembly's power to approve fare
provides an incentive for general cooperation by the transit company with the city branch as it attempts to establish coordinated
policies in mass transportation.

Public interest in urban transportation, particularly
fares and location of facilities, is lively.  Voters' meetings
frequently take stands on transit issues.  Considerable attention is paid by the city assembly to suggestions forwarded by
a large number of voters' meetings.  Problems of roads and
transit, together with housing, are those of most intense interest to the public and to local organizations of the Socialist

Alliance in Zagreb.  While fragmentation of responsibility in housing renders it difficult to channel resentment over housing problems, the Zagreb Electrical Tramway Corporation provides a clear target for public criticism.  The press gives extensive coverage to transportation problems, and its criticisms of existing services tend to reflect public feeling.

The political organizations--local committees of the League of Communists, the Socialist Alliance, and the trade unions--exert considerable influence over the company, particularly on personnel matters.  They, as well as the city transport unit, attempt to persuade the transit company to allow public interest, as they interpret it, to prevail over the company's particular interests.  Informal give-and-take between city authorities and the transit company are most intense in matters of planning and capital finance, which are discussed below, because transportation deficiencies are extremely visible in Zagreb.

## Transportation Problems

The inability of public services to keep up with rapid urban growth in Yugoslavia, as in other nations, is general. In the case of mass transportation in Zagreb, the inadequacy is simply felt more immediately by a greater number of people. It has two principal aspects.

The first is the restricted capacity of the existing transportation system.  Table 8 shows the increase in rolling stock for both trams and bus transportation during a recent eight-year period.

## TABLE 8

### Total Rolling Stock, Zagreb

| | Trams | | Buses | |
|---|---|---|---|---|
| | Motor Coaches | Coaches | Motor Coaches | Coaches |
| 1956 | 100 | 90 | 39 | - |
| 1957 | 109 | 90 | 54 | - |
| 1958 | 110 | 90 | 56 | - |
| 1959 | 120 | 100 | 66 | - |
| 1960 | 129 | 100 | 79 | 8 |
| 1961 | 135 | 109 | 89 | 9 |
| 1962 | 140 | 129 | 118 | 9 |
| 1963 | 142 | 132 | 119 | 8 |

In spite of this increase of about 40 per cent in trams
and more than 200 per cent in buses, the ratio of passengers
to capacity in mass-transportation vehicles is not improving
because of the population increase, new industrial development, and extension of the area serviced.  Overcrowding,
especially at peak hours, prevails throughout the system.
Roughly 75 per cent of all person-trips on an average day are
journeys to and from work in Zagreb during the morning and
evening rush hours.  About 65 per cent of all trips to and from
work in the "central-city area" are by mass transportation.
Private motor vehicle travel still accounts for only about 12
per cent of these work trips, while other private modes, such
as bicycles and walking, account for about 23 per cent. [10]  In
addition to the inadequacies of rolling stock, which are obvious
to the public at large, people engaged in and responsible for
the operation of transportation services complain about the lack
of fixed facilities such as repair shops, spare parts, and opportunities for specialized training of personnel.

The second aspect of transportation deficiencies in Zagreb is the design of the network, which is not adapted for modern requirements of speed, safety, and minimum obstruction
to city life.  Most of the existing tram lines pass through older
portions of the city, where streets are narrow and winding.  It
is precisely in these parts of the city that the tram tracks are
not separated from the rest of the road.  With increasing motor-
vehicle traffic, double tram lines in already narrow streets
impede traffic flow.  The average commercial speed of trams
and buses has not improved in the last five years.  In 1963,
this average speed was 9.3 miles per hour for trams and 12.2
miles per hour for buses.

According to estimates by the transport unit of the city
government, 95 per cent of the urban-area population is within
comparatively convenient distance of public transportation lines.
The areas not served, such as the hills in the northwest section of the area, are sparsely populated.  If this percentage is
differentiated for the central-city area and for the rest of the
urban area, however, nearly 100 per cent coverage is obtained
for the first and about 70 per cent for the second.  In 1957,
only about 10 per cent of persons employed in Zagreb lived
outside the metropolitan city limits, and these traveled up to
30 miles.  Commuters traveling in these patterns must depend

upon the automobile and the railroad for service. [11] Construction of South Zagreb on the right bank of the Sava River will require new transportation routes.

Finally, the railroad system is a serious source of transportation problems in Zagreb. The railroad is one of the few public services in Zagreb in which republic and federal governments are directly involved. It is not surprising that it is in this sphere that difficulties are encountered in arriving at agreement on projects; similar problems of intergovernmental relationships are familiar in other cities around the world where several levels of government are involved in project financing and authorization.

The railroad track, built in 1862, traverses the city in an east-west direction, constituting a barrier to development on the south, toward the river. Its crossings in the center of the city impede traffic, and its yards and workshops occupy prime land. The growth of the city's population and economy has led to a clash of interests between city authorities and the railroad system. The urban plan, in its draft stages, called for raised tracks through the city for passenger travel and diversion of freight traffic to new tracks and a station on the perimeter, as well as construction of a new terminal.

The railroad organization is a national federation of enterprises subject to supervision of the republic government. The high costs of the proposed work in Zagreb must be shared by federal, republic, and city authorities, as well as by the railroad enterprise. Controversy has centered on the relative shares of each and on project design. City authorities proposed a design that they considered desirable in terms of long-range urban-development goals, while the other participants-- not directly interested in the city itself--have urged less costly alternatives. To date, work on removing the tracks from street level is under way, however.

### Transportation Planning

Planning of local mass transportation in Zagreb is closely coordinated with urban-development planning generally. There is a continuing working relationship between the transit company and the department of building, communal and housing affairs on one side, and the city planning authorities on the other. This relationship has worked fairly well. The main complaint of the transportation authorities has been that the city and communal assemblies delayed so long in adopting a binding urban plan that would provide a dependable basis for their shorter-term plans and programs.  A main reason for the delay was the unresolved controversy over the railroad projects.  Largely because of this stalemate, the plan presented to the city assembly in 1953 was not adopted until 1966, although the planning authorities in 1955 undertook a detailed analysis of various proposals for solving the railway problem.

The urban plan provides in general for an increase of about 350 per cent in the area devoted to roads and parking lots and of over 200 per cent in the area devoted to railroad roadbeds (see Table 6).  An increase in transit passengers of 110 per cent is expected by 1993, but a detailed long-range transit plan is not completed.

The major program for the development of the transit services in Zagreb was included in the draft seven-year plan for Zagreb (1964-70).  The transportation section of this plan was based on an extrapolation of past trends.  Increase in bus passengers of about 10 per cent per year would bring the number of bus passengers from about 106,000 a day in 1963 to about 206,000 in 1970.  The number of tram passengers is expected to increase at a slower rate, from 503,000 a day in 1963 to 620,000 in 1970.  These calculations are based on the further assumption that the present increase in the use of private motor vehicles will continue.  The plan provides for extending tram lines into newly developed parts of the city, particularly on the southern bank of the river; extending bus lines and increasing the frequency of bus service; improving the standards of comfort for passengers; and improving maintenance of both roadbed and rolling stock. [12]

The transit program was prepared by the transit company in collaboration with the transport and roads branch of the city government and was incorporated by the Zagreb Planning Institute into the draft seven-year plan.  The transportation program had been discussed by the then-existing Council for Transportation and Communication of the city assembly. It was also discussed in conjunction with the total seven-year plan by the assembly's Committee on Planning and Finance. The transit part of the plan was adopted by the assembly.

Detailed plans for capital investment and financing of
the program were then prepared by the transit company and
sent to the city administration for technical control and
coordination with other requirements of the city's annual
plans. The process of coordination is informal, as investment decisions by the transit company are not subject to formal approval by local authorities. These programs refrained
from impinging on the subjects still under discussion in
connection with the railroad and long-term urban-development
plan. The city planning authorities are influential throughout
these processes, but unsettled questions of urban design did
hamstring transit programming.

### Investment in Transportation Expansion

Under the transit plan, both operating costs and capital
investments are to be financed from increased fares--a highly
controversial policy. Over past years, an increasing part of
capital costs has been covered by fare revenues. Total capital
expenditure on the services of the Zagreb Electrical Tramway
and the one City Railway line from 1959 to 1963 was 6.4 billion
dinars. About 22 per cent was derived from long-term loans,
cash outlays from the city budget, and contributions by various
enterprises in the urban area, particularly organizations on
the city's outskirts that wished to induce the public transportation system to extend its lines into their vicinity. About 4.9
billion dinars came from fare income and tax rebates by the
city government. The total subsidy in tax rebates and cash
outlays from the city totaled about 50 per cent of the capital
investment over the five-year period.

Whether most, if not all, capital expenditure for transportation should be derived from operating revenues has been
much debated in the city assembly. The majority is willing to
continue tax rebates but is loath to continue cash outlays, which
must come from the city budget, as apportionment among the
communes would be exceedingly difficult. While the transit
company is in principle independent in investment decisions,
the city's control over fares, subsidies, and loans makes the
normal decision-making procedure a public one. The debate
is followed closely by the public, which considers transportation
fares an important item in family budgets. The three parties
to the debate on financing--the public, the transit company,
and the city--have different short-term interests. The public
and the city would like to pay as little as possible, and the

corporation to get as much as possible from both. The opposition of the public has succeeded in deferring fare increases until recently, when transit fare raises were passed by the city assembly in the wake of general price increases.

If the fare increases prove adequate to finance the improvements and extensions called for in the seven-year plan, plan implementation will depend mainly on operating decisions and will not require repeated annual investment commitments by city authorities. But if further fare increases are required, continuing opposition by the public may either interfere with the pace of plan implementation or require city authorities to re-examine the long-term credit policies.

## Interagency Relationships

In summary, although the bulk of transit services in Zagreb are the responsibility of a single agency--the Zagreb Electrical Tramway Corporation, which is in theory independent of general government--transportation operations and particularly new developments result from an ongoing interplay among the transit company, city authorities, and the public and political organizations. An example may serve to clarify this process. As has been mentioned, one of the main difficulties with transportation in Zagreb is that most of the tram lines pass through narrow streets of the old center along with motor traffic, pedestrians, and general bustle. An additional main east-west tram line with separate roadbed existed, however, south of the railroad tracks. As the two major parallel lines were connected only at one western point, the southern line did not provide access to the center of the city for people living or working in the expanding southeastern industrial sector. Building a junction of the two parallel lines in the east would have the double advantage of improving eastern connection and of providing an alternative east-west route to the one that ran through the clogged center. Construction of this junction required building crossings at different levels for railway and tram lines and opening a new street across a slum and industrial area.

The major proponents of this improvement were the roads and transport branch of the city administration and the Zagreb Electrical Tramway Corporation. Support of the Zagreb Institute for Urban Planning was obtained when it agreed that the proposal was in keeping with its conceptions for the long-term

development. (Such agreement had not been easily forthcoming with respect to specific transit-improvement proposals.) On the other hand, city financial authorities pro-
tested that too large an expenditure was required for what was
a piecemeal improvement of the transportation system. The
argument was made that if the present draft urban plan was
implemented, railway traffic would be removed from its present path altogether, which would obviate the necessity for
building different level crossings. In addition, a large liquor
factory in the path of the projected line opposed the proposal.
The stalemate was broken when the city's then-existing Council for Transportation and Communications was able to enlist
the powerful support of the new industrial enterprises in the
southeastern part of the city and to overcome opposition by
proving that different level crossings would have to be built
whatever the ultimate solution of the railway problem. Indem-
nification was offered to the liquor factory. In 1961, the city
assembly adopted the plan for the new tram line, which was
forwarded to it by its Council for Transportation and Communications. Work on the project began immediately and was completed in 1962.

There are no active proposals in Zagreb for major organizational or administrative changes for transportation, except for integration of the City Railway Corporation, which
operates one specialized line, into the Zagreb Electric Tramways Corporation. The central administrative problems in
transportation seem to be, on the one hand, delay in achieving
consensus on the railroad projects and, on the other hand, unresolved issues in the relationship between city government and
transit company.

In keeping with general policies for functional decentralization, there has been progressive disengagement of the city
from its primary responsibility in mass passenger transportation. With the increasing operational and financial independence of the one big transportation agency, the Zagreb Electrical Tramways Corporation, the role of the city may wither, a
tendency reinforced by the many conflicting claims on the city's
resources in men and material. It seems questionable to some
local observers to let a public utility not only operate the service but also decide general policy. Some local interests question whether the general atmosphere of informal cooperation
is enough to enable the city to discharge its responsibility.

Since most local mass-transportation services are concentrated in the Zagreb Electrical Tramways Corporation, and since the department of building, communal, and housing affairs operates as a central clearinghouse for transportation, housing, water, and other physical urban services, problems of operating coordination have not been serious in Zagreb, although they may become so with increasing autonomy of the operating agencies and loosening up of the planning system.

## PRIMARY AND SECONDARY EDUCATION

Under policies of the Constitution and the national political leadership, education is to be public but not governmental, a distinction that underlies the whole economic and social structure toward which Yugoslavia is moving. Accordingly, schools should be managed independently by their teaching staffs, with the active participation of interested community groups. They should have financial resources independent of government budgets. In so far as feasible, even inspection and supervision should be in the hands of functionally autonomous organs--institutes for schools--rather than in the hands of general government line agencies. At present, the schools are autonomous working organizations supervised by local governments and financed by special school funds.

The Yugoslavia Constitution guarantees free and compulsory elementary education for eight years, and makes the local community responsible for providing "the material and other prerequisites for the creation and functioning of schools and other institutions for the education of citizens and for furthering their activities."

Prior to World War II, education was compulsory for four years only, and there were several types of elementary schools--eight-year schools, four-year schools--and "lower secondary schools," which provided a second four years of elementary education. All have been transformed into uniform eight-year schools. A variety of secondary schools is maintained:

1. Gymnasiums, providing four years of general secondary education preparatory to university education.

2.  Four- to five-year technical schools.

3.  Four-year schools of administration and office management.

4.  Medical schools for sanitation technicians and nurses, offering two- to four-year courses.

5.  Elementary teacher-training schools with four-year programs.

6.  Industrial schools providing skill training for two to four years.

7.  Arts schools offering from four to ten years of general education.

In the first five-year plan period beginning in 1947, technical education was stressed in secondary curriculums as a necessary corollary to industrialization.  Thereafter, increasing ascendancy of the humanities was based on the policy that everyone should receive a general education sufficient to enable him to pursue higher education if he wished and to enjoy the world's cultural heritage.  As a consequence, the introduction of general education courses into technical and other specialized secondary schools has exceeded that in most countries.  In general, the curriculums of Yugoslav schools are highly varied; some educational interests consider them somewhat overburdened.

Private schools, limited to those for religious servants, are private organizations under no obligation as to their programs.

At present in Zagreb, educational facilities are sufficient to accommodate all children of elementary-school age, although crowding is experienced.  In 1961, over 92 per cent (54,488 out of 58,907) of urban children from seven to fifteen years old were regularly attending school.  Family difficulties and marginal social-welfare problems account for existing nonattendance.

Secondary-school enrollment in the urban area increased by almost 40 per cent (from 19,584 to 27,196) between 1960

and 1965. (The parallel increase in elementary-school enrollment was 11 per cent.) An increasing proportion of children
are continuing into secondary education.

Moderate overcrowding is reflected in class sizes ex-
ceeding the local standard, which is 25 to 30 for elementary
schools and 20 to 25 for secondary schools, and in multiple
shifts. The current average class size in the "central city"
area of Zagreb, according to the city education authorities,
is 35.3 in elementary schools, 36.1 in gymnasiums, and 30.2
in other secondary schools. While the capacity of education
facilities has not limited attendance, it has affected the quality
of teaching. The city department of education estimates that
150 new primary-school classrooms and 130 new secondary-
school classrooms are needed to accommodate presently eligible students in standard class sizes. To accommodate eligible children in 1975, taking into consideration increases in
secondary-school attendance, some 530 new elementary classrooms and 860 new secondary classrooms will be required.
Hence, the pressure on the system to maintain rapid expansion
is considerable.

The record of expansion in the urban area for 1959 through
1963 shows 3,851 million dinars invested to establish 278 new
elementary classrooms, and 2,655 million to create 132 new
secondary classrooms. That rate of expansion is adequate to
meet 1975 targets for elementary facilities but would have to
be more than tripled for secondary schools.

Although the teacher shortage is severe in the rural sector of the Zagreb District, it is not serious in urban Zagreb.
Out of about 4,000 teachers in the urban area, roughly 120 to
160 need additional education to fully meet the formal requirements. Teachers of the first four grades of elementary school
are required to have a diploma from a teacher-training college,
which provides two years of study beyond secondary school.
Teachers of the last four elementary grades and of secondary
classes must have a university degree (four years of higher
education). After five years in service, teachers must pass
an examination administered by the Republic of Croatia in order
to continue. No temporary permits are issued.

Most of the prewar teachers have been retained. While
the higher government and political organizations have sufficient influence to prevent the content of teaching from

conflicting directly with the fundamental policies on which
Yugoslav society is based, teachers and local community interests have significant controlling powers in local education.

## Social Management

Each school, primary or secondary, in Zagreb is an
autonomous working organization under control of a school
board that is composed predominantly of the school faculty,
together with representatives of the communal assembly and
of neighborhood organizations and enterprises. A teachers'
council and its executive board oversee day-to-day management, which the director carries out. The school director is
appointed by the school board from candidates named by a
nominating committee on which the communal assembly and
the teachers' council are equally represented. School personnel and operations are the responsibility of the school board
and the teachers' council.

This organizational form demonstrates the Yugoslav concept of "social management" in community facilities. The
teachers' council parallels a workers' council in an economic
enterprise. Supervision and policy control by a social-
management organ--the school board--that includes representatives of the community served is superimposed because of the
essentially social function of the school. Each school receives
earmarked resources for its independent budget from the local
school fund. Thus, decentralization of formal structure has
been carried down to the lowest educational level--the individual school. In practice, however, the role of government,
particularly city authorities, is still important in local education.

## Government Education Agencies

Education is the direct responsibility of the republic in
Yugoslavia. The national government has prescribed only the
common principles to be followed in educational systems, and
its Secretariat for Education and Culture and Federal Board of
Education offer advice, albeit influential advice, and technical
assistance.

The Croatian assembly and executive council, utilizing
the republic education department, prescribe standard

curriculums for schools and approve textbooks.  Individual
schools can amend the standard curriculums if they feel local
conditions so require, with approval of the republic department.  The republic department also plans the network of
secondary schools.  Planning new elementary schools in the
urban area is the role of the city authorities.  In principle,
the communes have direct responsibility for supervising
operations in elementary education, and the city, in secondary
education.  The city also has coordinating powers with respect
to elementary education.

The city department of education and culture is responsible politically to the city assembly's Chamber on Education
and Culture.  It is responsible to the secretary of the city for
daily conduct of administration.  The department, like other
Zagreb government units, doubles as a district unit and a
city administration.

The department of education and culture includes a division of education and physical culture, a division of planning
and finance, and a unit for culture.  The first division is subdivided into a unit for general secondary schools, a unit for
technical and special schools, and a unit for elementary
schools.  Due to the independent powers of schools over appointments, the department has insignificant influence on
school personnel.

The department exercises substantial city responsibilities.
It plans construction of schools--including elementary schools--
in the city, these plans being integrated into general city economic and social plans.  It establishes and has constructed new
secondary schools within the framework of the Croatian plan
for the development of secondary schools and with the approval
of the republic executive council.  It also establishes special
schools, such as those for blind, deaf, and retarded children.
The city department has the authority to certify that an individual school meets legal requirements and may begin to operate, and authority to order a school to close on grounds that
it fails to meet legal requirements.  Also, it determines the
over-all enrollment magnitudes for various types of schools.
It supervises the legality of secondary-school operation and
"coordinates" such supervision of elementary schools by the
communes.  Inspection is carried out by the Zagreb Institute
for Schools, which the department oversees.  The department
also provides administrative services for the school fund.

Finally, it is responsible for analyzing the state of education and educational problems, and submitting appropriate proposals to the city assembly, particularly the Chamber of Education and Culture.

The Zagreb Institute for Schools gradually obtained independent status from the city government. In 1966, it was permitted its own management council. Previously, its director had been appointed by and was responsible to the city assembly but reported in matters of administration to the head of the department of education and culture. It is organized into three functional inspection sections: for schools of general education, for subject-matter instruction, and for technical and specialized education. The Institute's responsibilities are mainly to supervise the educational performance of the schools, a duty discharged formerly by school-inspection units within the city department of education. Separation of the inspection services from the general department is meant to be a step toward more complete decentralization of education, increasing autonomy from the government bureaucracy. The institute includes a considerable number of high-ranking professional specialists in education who engage in applied research.

The sections or division of education in the urban communes of Zagreb are the administrative organs of the communal assemblies for school matters. As schools fall under the constitutional definition of autonomous working organizations, legally prescribed government contacts with them--such as participation in the nominating committees and on the school boards--are by the commune. The commune education units are line agencies with directors appointed by the communal assembly. Their charter duties with respect to elementary schools are analogous to those of the city department of education with respect to secondary schools. Official city policy on division of duties between city and communes is that the commune units should be responsible for supervising school operations while the city department plays a coordinating role. This pattern is not practicable at present due to the limited capacity of communal administration. As a result, the commune education units perform what functions they can, under an informal arrangement with the city department. The city and commune charters are sufficiently elastic to make this adjustment possible. The territorial division of responsibility is highly contingent upon solutions to financial issues in local education.

## Educational Finance

While city and commune education departments are supported by general tax revenues in the local budgets, [13] school
operating budgets and capital investment in education are financed by separate funds--the school funds.  These funds were
established at both the city and commune levels with the aim
of freeing the schools from government budgets.  They are
organized according to the principles of federal basic law and
decree of 1960 and 1961.  Establishing the city school fund
required approval of the Republic of Croatia Assembly, while
the communes were free to organize the funds without approval.

The funds, which have their own management boards appointed by the local assembly, receive revenues from earmarked taxes and local authority budgets.  The city assembly
divides education revenues between city and commune school
funds.

Moneys are allocated by contract from the funds to the
various schools to meet costs in their lump-sum budget.  In
addition, the funds finance capital investment.  However, the
local assembly must approve the fund's finance plan, and
legal formulas provide criteria for allocation (number of students, age of building, etc.).  For school-construction and
other capital outlays, a fund's management board commits its
resources within the framework of a school-development plan
adopted by the local assembly.

The commune funds are responsible for financing elementary schools, and the city fund for secondary schools.
Through 1965, however, the city fund had provided the bulk of
funds for both, the ratio between the city fund and total commune funds being about 7 to 3. [14]

In order to maximize the independence of schools and
minimize government interference, increasing autonomy of
the school funds was called for in the early 1960's.  The city
school fund is managed as a dependency of the department of
education, however.  The degree of freedom that the funds
can enjoy is a function of the stability and independence of
their sources of revenue.  Practically all depended upon
local-government subsidies to supplement their earmarked
tax revenues, and in 1965 federal law made local-government
budgets ultimately responsible for education finance.  The

general subsidy to the city fund has represented a heavy financial charge, consuming from year to year nearly the entire city-budget reserve fund (211 million dinars in 1964).

Some Yugoslav educational specialists have advocated
a system of school-fund financing similar to that for social-
security funds.  Each year the Federal Assembly votes the
percentage contribution of enterprises and local governments
to the social-security funds in order to meet expenditures
forecast by the Social Security Administration.  Some voices
have been raised, especially after introduction of lump-sum
budgets for schools, for introduction of tuition fees.  But this
is excluded for elementary schools by the constitutional guarantee and is unlikely to be accepted for secondary schools in
view of prevailing ideas and traditions.  A federal law of
1965 settled these issues in favor of local-government financing.

The problem of delimiting responsibility for education
between the city and the communes has been compounded by
financial difficulties.  The communes have been neither willing
nor able to fulfill the role assigned to them, particularly because they would have to spend large parts of their budgets on
schools.

Hence, there are strong arguments for keeping the city
and its department of education in effective charge of education.
Full development of the communal powers might make it difficult to coordinate educational development itself and with
other aspects of urban development, and complicate the implementation of comprehensive educational policy.  The coordinating tasks of the city are complex with the existing degree of functional decentralization.  For example, industrial
secondary schools that train students in advanced skills are
often created on the initiative of industrial enterprises and
tend to disregard restrictions imposed by city educational
authorities.

It has been proposed that Zagreb proceed with functional
decentralization in education but with a strong central body
responsible directly to the city assembly to undertake educational planning, financing, and supervision.  Such a central
body might include representatives from the schools and have

greater independence from general administration than the
school fund and institute presently have.   The prospects for
greater territorial decentralization--that is transfer of actual
functions from the city to the communes--are far dimmer.


## NOTES TO CHAPTER 5

1.   In practice, commune and city authorities have considerable influence in selecting the Water System director.
Candidacies are discussed by the workers' council with local
political leadership, particularly city and commune committees of the League of Communists and Socialist Alliance.   The
political leadership cannot impose a candidate against the
wishes of the workers' council, but neither can the council
choose a candidate who is unacceptable to the political leaders.

2.   Authorization for construction and use of wells by
individual enterprises is issued with the building permit by the
commune in which the enterprise is situated; while such enterprises are formally required to install water meters in order
to allow control of the quantity of water used, this requirement
is often honored in the breach.

3.   Sewerage services are provided by an independent
enterprise entitled "Sewers," which is a public corporation in
much the same sense as the Water System.   The city water and
sewer subunit serves as a coordinating clearinghouse for both
the water and sewerage enterprises.

4.   The new price structure is as follows:   120 dinars per
cubic meter for economic enterprises, 80 dinars per cubic meter for public agencies and institutions, 40 dinars per cubic meter for households, and 20 dinars per cubic meter for public
uses by general government units.

5.   Of this, 40. 6 per cent went to households, 37. 1 per
cent to economic enterprises, 18. 7 per cent to public agencies
and institutions, and 3. 6 per cent for general public uses.

6.   One should recall, however, that the average value
of total income, including benefits, is really double the salaries.

7.    Standard dwelling units in Zagreb are those with nineteen or more square meters of floor space per occupant; built with specified permanent materials; with termic and acoustical insulation; and with running water, sewer connection, toilet, and electricity.  The urban-development program calls for raising standards to twenty square meters per occupant.

8.    In addition, the revenue accounts of the housing funds included the capital contributed by cooperatives and enterprises for construction on their behalf.

9.    Before the new system was instituted, the average monthly rent for a two-room dwelling of 50 square meters was 6,076 dinars, roughly 15 per cent of the average monthly salary of employed persons in the urban area.

The calculation of this average rent is illustrated in the following example:

|   |   | Dinars |
|---|---|---|
| 1. | Building construction price per square meter | 72,903 |
| 2. | Construction price of the dwelling (50 square meters) | 3,645,150 |
| 3. | Monthly depreciation (the above figure divided by 1,200) | 3,038 |
| 4. | Monthly charge for maintenance and administration | 3,038 |
| 5. | Total monthly rent | 6,076 |

10.    These percentages are computed from estimates given by officials of the traffic-control service (police) at the main points of entrance into the central-city area.

11.    See Stanko Žuljic: "O dnevnim kretanjima radne snage u zagreba,"Geografski Glasnik, 1957, pp. 135-47.

12.    The total capital expenditure needed for implementing the seven-year transportation program is as follows:

|   | Million Dinars |
|---|---|
| Total | 16,200 |
| Rolling Stock | 7,409 |
| Rights of Way | 4,268 |
| Fixed Facilities | 4,523 |

13.    In 1964, the section of the city budget covering the city department of education and the Zagreb Institute for Schools was 22. 5 million dinars and those of the education units in the nine communes totaled 27. 6 million dinars.

14.    The city department of education and culture estimated total school-fund expenditure in the urban area in 1964 at 7, 750 million dinars for elementary- and secondary-school budgets and 2, 500 million dinars in capital investment.

CHAPTER **6** ISSUES OF URBAN
GOVERNMENT

Zagreb differs from the other urban areas studied in
this series in that the structure of its local government and
its organization for public services have not developed piecemeal through history nor been adjusted haphazardly to political and technical exigencies. The organizational characteristics of Zagreb's urban services have been explicitly designed in recent years not only as a means of meeting service
needs of rapid urban growth, but also--and more emphasis
has been put on this aspect--as a means of achieving certain
social values, predominantly those expressed in functional
and territorial decentralization, debureaucratization, and
citizen participation.

Thus, greater uniformity of administrative patterns is
found among various clusters of public activity in Zagreb than
in other urban areas, where arrangements vary considerably
from service to service. In all four types of activity examined closely in this study--housing, water supply, transportation, and education--federal law supplemented by republic
law provides the framework of regulation, both as to output
standards and as to organizational forms and procedures. In
all four, however, essential planning, financing, and operating responsibilities rest with the intra-urban authorities in
the city and communes. As a result of efforts to achieve functional decentralization, each service is provided by a special
agency that has independence of varying intensity from general
government. The Water System and Zagreb Electrical Tramways are examples of public corporations with formal and informal ties to local government. Schools are autonomous
working organizations, with special mechanisms for social
management that represent citizen-users. Housing enterprises, school funds, and planning institutes are examples of
other types of functional agencies separate from general government line administration.

The internal departments of general government are left with duties of coordinating, supervising, and developing comprehensive policies for submission to the assembly. These duties are performed by the city department of building, housing, and communal affairs for water, housing, and transportation. This concentration of urban-service responsibility in one department facilitates interservice coordination at the operating stages, for the department functions as a communication focal point. The department of education and culture has a larger decision-making role, as the school funds and schools themselves are subject to greater regulation than water and transit corporations. It is understandable that a different mode of functional decentralization is reached in education, for it differs in kind, having far more significant ramifications for the social system. In education, the social-policy aspects of decisions are more predominant than the technical aspects.

Common threads of fiscal policy run through all the major urban services in Zagreb. These include the efforts to maximize return from user charges and, where public funds are necessary, to derive them from functionally earmarked resources. An attempt is being made in water, housing, and transit services to have user charges cover not only operating costs but also capital investments. The general resources that flow into housing and schools have been for the most part from specially designated taxes that bypass the local-government budget, although local budget responsibility for schools was asserted in 1965.

Citizen discussion, influence of the political organizations, and in specific instances, influence of major economic enterprises are high in all the service areas examined.

Zagreb shares many problems with other urban areas of vastly different economic levels and governmental systems. Housing and transportation are the most strongly felt areas of deficiency in all the urban areas studied in this series. Difficulties in mobilizing capital investment for urban infrastructure at a rate concomitant with population growth and the needs of complex urban life are experienced in Zagreb as elsewhere. The response in Zagreb to large demands on capital resources has been an attempt to expand current revenues, particularly user charges. For a general policy, this is an unusual approach; for the most part, other cities depend upon higher-government grants and local-government borrowing for capital funds. Zagreb has the advantage of having set user charges for such services as water and transit at economic levels, whereas most urban areas have failed to collect them at a high enough rate to cover operating costs. The requirement that the local government meet the difference between operating costs and operating revenues if they do not approve economic fare structures is a useful mechanism for reconciling political and economic factors in setting prices. This mechanism is also used in Paris and Stockholm, but there the local governments have chosen in many cases to subsidize the services. While fare raises in Zagreb were somewhat disguised by general price increases due to inflation, in Paris they have been resisted explicitly by the government in order to hold down the cost-of-living index.

The scope and design of long-term future development is a major unresolved policy problem in Zagreb as in most urban areas of the world. Urban-development programs devised over the past fifteen to twenty years are based on a projection of present population trends in the urban area, which would move Zagreb toward the 1 million mark in the 1990's. Lately, however, that assumption has caused growing concern and criticism. Local critics argue that the optimum size of a city is near the 500,000 level. They maintain that a city of a million could not be conveniently accommodated within the present geographic center of Zagreb, which is protected by the mountains from the north winds. They hold that it would be demographically unsound to concentrate in one big city one-fourth of the projected population of the Republic of Croatia, and point out that at present prices every 1,000 new industrial workers require a public capital investment averaging about 10 billion dinars. The amount needed to provide industrial employment for 200,000 new people within the next five to thirty years would not be forthcoming, so that the present ratio of increase in urban population would result in a severe deterioration of present living standards in the city, an increase in unemployment, and creation of slums. On these grounds more and more voices in policy circles at urban and republic levels are favoring systematic limitation of immigration to the city. They suggest an energetic program of rural reconstruction throughout the republic in order to prevent flight from the land, a more comprehensive regional plan for parallel development of a number of smaller cities in northwest

Croatia in order to take the pressure off Zagreb, and construction of satellite settlements around Zagreb that would be
connected to the city by fast local transportation.

However, other officials, including the city's highest
executive officers, believe that it is necessary to prepare for
a continuing increase in Zagreb's population at the present
rates. They argue that it is not within the power of policy-
making to stop the growth of Zagreb or significantly reduce
the rate of increase. Even under the unlikely assumption that
the constitutional principle of free migration be abandoned,
the example of Moscow is cited to show the failure of systematic
and energetic administrative measures to limit immigration.
The experience of Milan is pointed out to illustrate that even
the growth of other urban centers in the immediate vicinity
has no appreciable influence on urban population growth. The
present structure of agriculture in Yugoslavia, entailing a high
proportion of hidden unemployment, will continue to motivate
migration to the cities. These officials feel, in fact, that
extrapolation of present trends into the future underestimates
the population increase, which is more likely to accelerate.
The development of Zagreb is increasingly a national rather
than a Croatian phenomenon; as one of the two major cities of
Yugoslavia, it is becoming a point of attraction for people from
the neighboring states of Slovenia and Bosnia-Hercegovina. Cer-
tainly the increase will severely strain the city's economic resources but this group maintains that employment will rise in the
tertiary sector (trade, services, administration and professions)
so the relationship between capital investment and new jobs
assumed by those who would restrict urban growth would not
hold.

In any case, it seems evident that under present conditions Zagreb will continue to grow. How these issues of long-
range urban planning are resolved will govern the timely com-
mitment of huge resources to provide the public infrastructure
to accommodate this growth.

This issue--to grow or not to grow--is a vital one in
most large urban areas of the world. Governments have tried
to limit the growth of Paris, Lodz (Poland), and Leningrad.
The engorgement of Lagos, Calcutta, Lima, Valencia (Vene-
zuela), and Casablanca with underserviced, low-income population is of serious concern. In most cases, the only feasible
answer is a compromise. Rapid urban growth is a universal

phenomenon, a concomitant of industrialization and economic development. Those who consider it inevitable are being proved right. But those who underscore the enormous public investments required and the balancing effects of developing counter-magnet urban centers also have a valid point.

The general patterns of migration and urbanization that so severely affect the burdens on urban administration are national phenomena, arising from economic changes, rural productivity, pricing and tax policies, national transportation networks, and sometimes even international events. For the most part, these are outside the influence of local authorities; the responsibility must rest with national policy.

In any case, the examples of both Paris and Lodz show that limiting investment in large cities, rather than stemming the tide of migration, merely widens the gap between public needs and public services.

Local-government responsibilities and powers in Zagreb have expanded rapidly in proportion to urban problems, in direct contrast to the trends in most urban areas of the world, where the roles of all levels of government are increasing, with those of state and national authorities growing faster. This contrast may be partly explained by the fact that the administrative jurisdiction of the Zagreb urban area has grown progressively larger and embraces all the territory needed for planning long-term urban development, financing and providing regional services, and coordinating urban activities. A strong metropolitan jurisdiction meets some of the problems of urban growth that in other areas are met by state- or national-government activity. The government of Zagreb, in its double role of city and district, has at its disposal all the territory necessary to organize not only the foreseeable growth of the urban complex but also its regional communications network, supply systems, and recreational resources. At the same time, it has adequate powers to organize common services, to coordinate local activities, and to stimulate inter-communal cooperation.

Throughout the world, growth of central powers in local services has accompanied urbanization for several reasons: the national importance of large cities; the scale of urban investments that requires central-government resources; the technical nature of many urban problems, which heightens dependence on better-staffed higher-government civil service; and finally, evident needs for area-wide action and coordination that are not met adequately by small local units within the metropolis. Centralization is merely one of several possible administrative responses to these factors, however. Others include metropolitan organization and planning, strengthening local financial resources and personnel capabilities, and increasing the size of municipal units.

While Zagreb has run counter to centralization trends, it has made all three of these other responses. First, although several of the other urban areas studied are moving toward enlarging urban municipal units, Yugoslavia is far ahead of them; the communes in Zagreb are 20,000 or more in population. Second, local capital resources in Zagreb have expanded and become greater in relation to national investment than those in other cities where capital finance engages higher government to a large degree. And while the growth in local powers has put considerable strain on local personnel in Yugoslavia, this is not a severe problem in Zagreb, which has been able to recruit high talent into public service and to organize effective personnel-training programs. Third, while metropolitan mechanisms for planning and ad hoc cooperation or regional services are developing in many urban areas, Zagreb and a handful of others have full-fledged metropolitan government.

The last two developments--metropolitan organization and strengthening of local capabilities--interact to relieve pressure on higher government to meet urban problems. Casablanca, Davao, and Valencia, for example, have government jurisdictions of metropolitan scale. Without funds and legal powers to cope with major urban problems, however, these do not alter basic patterns of centralized administration. Ultimately, of course, the strength of local and metropolitan authorities depends upon the willingness of higher government to relinquish resources and operating responsibilities. This the Yugoslav Government has done to a remarkable degree (although some local officials feel that resources are slower in coming than responsibilities). Undoubtedly, the degree of political unity provides a basis for administrative decentralization.

Of course, higher government in Yugoslavia maintains certain controls over local-government activity, as do higher governments in all the areas studied. For Zagreb, however, higher-government controls consist mainly in broad legal, financial, and policy regulation, without detailed, day-to-day administrative supervision or approval of local decisions. This contrasts with the situation in even Stockholm and Toronto (among the more decentralized of our other case studies), where certain classes of local decisions must be approved by higher government and discretionary supervision is exercised over certain local-government activity. In addition, national and republic governments in Zagreb do not directly operate or execute any major urban services or improvement projects, which they do in most areas. Nor is there in Zagreb a hierarchy of administration under which local agencies take instructions and directions from higher agencies, as in Lodz and Leningrad.

The advantage of the Yugoslav system, as seen in Zagreb, is that decision-making can be focused within the urban area while the control of higher governments is adequate to protect national policies and interests. The centralization of the political organizations in Yugoslavia, as well as the interlocking system of plans, aids the national government in achieving general policy harmony, therefore rendering feasible a high degree of administrative decentralization. In many urban areas in developing countries, comprehensive plans and policies have not been developed and accepted to such an extent; neither is political stability as great. Therefore, detailed supervision and interference by higher government is considered necessary in order to protect national and regional interests.

Administration in Zagreb remains, of course, constrained by national policies. Resolution of national issues, such as directions of economic reform, has underlain recent changes in the planning system and in housing administration, for example. The autonomy of public-service organizations, such as school funds and public-service corporations, has fluctuated both with national law and local factors.

One method for control of local-government activities in Zagreb is particularly relevant to problems experienced in other areas; that is, the system of financial control. Local fiscal transactions are handled through the national bank branches, and the Social Accounting Service assures regularity and legality in the handling of funds by both local governments and independent corporations. A parallel is found in France, where local-government financial transactions, once authorized by local executives, are executed by a municipal treasurer who is an employee of the national Finance Ministry. Moreover, financial inspection is carried out in France by a separate national corps that is comparable in concept to the Social Accounting Service. However, France has the additional controls of national-government audit and budget approval, which are not applied in Zagreb.

In many areas, including Zagreb, local interests have opposed metropolitan organization and assumption of powers, in defense of their prerogatives. But if the only alternatives are expanded participation of central governments or helplessness in the face of mounting urban problems, the freedom and power to act of intra-urban interests as a whole would be better protected by area-wide organization.

It is no cure-all, of course. Even with large communes and a metropolitan tier of government, Zagreb is faced with certain administrative problems connected with territorial decentralization and metropolitan coordination. The division of the city into urban communes and the legal powers of communes within the framework of the emerging Yugoslav system of government have been accompanied by obvious difficulties. There is a widespread feeling that administration in Zagreb has become unnecessarily cumbersome and is not as efficient as it might be. In assessing the various factors contributing to this state of affairs, opinions are divided--for the most part, between city officials and commune officials. In city policy-making circles, the emerging opinion is that the main source of difficulties in administering the urban area is the very existence of the communes. The specific arguments are manifold. First, the total number of employees of city and communal special authorities and government has increased more than fourfold since the war, faster than the size of the city and the level of services. Part of the increase is said to be "dead weight," caused by the proliferation of the administrative machineries of the communes. The average time needed for administrative transactions has increased; often procedures on a proposal must be carried through both city and commune levels or through more than one commune. It is difficult to achieve unified policy, given the present status of the urban communes (for example, the communes have statutory prerogatives to control enterprises and organizations of general importance to the whole city).

A plan is under discussion to consolidate the nine urban communes of Zagreb into a single commune. [1] An alternative proposal would retain two tiers but amalgamate the lower level into three urban communes. Similar alternatives were raised before a royal commission examining metropolitan Toronto during 1965. It adopted a compromise solution, reducing the thirteen lower-tier municipalities to six.

On the surface, such changes in Zagreb run counter to the concept of the communes as natural communities of citizens and working organizations, and basic units of both government and society. Defenders of the existing communes doubt that unsatisfactory administration can be wholly ascribed to the existence of communes. They argue that their disappearance would unnecessarily centralize city bureaucracy and would destroy the communes' achievements in bringing day-to-day city administration nearer to the citizens. Proponents of the one-city view answer that opportunities for political participation are considerably more diversified than twelve years ago, when the communes were the only forms through which citizens could influence community decisions.

The most extreme defenders of the communes hold that city government for the urban area is altogether unnecessary, that it would be sufficient if the urban communes could establish common services for the whole urban area managed by delegates from the communes. [2]

These arguments are difficult to resolve, because underlying them are conflicts of interest between the existing authorities, as well as between two different public policies--both considered valid in Yugoslav theory. The argument tends to take the form of controversy between political principle and pragmatic administrative considerations. Creation of the urban communes in Zagreb in 1953, over the explicit opposition of some officials, was a victory of the political principle that the commune should be the arena of direct democracy, for which it was felt the City of Zagreb was too large. It has proved difficult over time to steer a middle course between domination of the commune governments by the city administration--which has occurred in matters of finance--and local interference with the discharge of city responsibilities as an urban government.

This examination of urban administration in Zagreb has shown that practical considerations of finance and administration have resulted in the city government's playing a dominant role in urban administration.  In all major service areas, the role of the second tier of urban government looms far larger than that of the communes.  A certain amount of duplication of effort and particularism is a byproduct of the present division of powers, but the relationship of the city and commune has proved flexible and is as yet unsettled. Undoubtedly, there will be at minimum some shifting of functions between the two levels in a search for pragmatic solutions.

Another major aspect of administrative problems in the Zagreb system involves coordination of enterprises, institutes, and various public-service units.  Special authorities for urban services have proliferated in many nations.  In Yugoslavia, their growth in number and independence is constitutionally based.  Public policy in Yugoslavia, in contrast to many other areas, explicitly favors single-purpose (rather than multi-purpose) special authorities, for they are designed to deconcentrate administrative power rather than to consolidate it. In the other urban areas examined in this series, special area-wide agencies are generally considered mechanisms for concentrating functions previously scattered among small units.

There are other interesting contrasts with Yugoslav theory relating to special authorities.  In many multi-party nations, public authorities separated from general government have been created for particular urban services explicitly to isolate them from political influence.  Critics of this practice complain they are thereby isolated from democratic government. In Zagreb, however, special authorities are used to increase the influence of represented groups--particularly of employees in an institution and in some cases of neighborhood groups. (This is similar to the rationale for separate local school boards in the United States and Canada, for example.)  The influence of political organizations is considered proper both in general government and in special authorities.

Questions are open in Zagreb, however, as to how much policy control general city government should maintain over public corporations and other independent organizations and how they can be effectively coordinated.  In Zagreb, as in

other areas, complaints are raised that public-service corporations tend to formulate and pursue their own interests,
which may not always correspond with general public interests.

Some specific controls of local government over public
corporations in Zagreb (such as approval of prices and participation in selection of the director) are utilized to sensitize
the agencies to the public interest, as interpreted by representative organs of government. For the most part, however,
Zagreb city authorities favor achieving coordination more by
communication than by control. They propose to utilize
special coordinating bodies separate from general government,
such as the institutes of health, welfare, education, and planning. In the future, these may be linked up to the agencies
they are coordinating by having their management bodies composed of delegates from the operating agencies. The hope is
that a structurally fragmented administrative system might be
organically unified by overlapping membership and by maintaining a pluralistic planning process.

Efforts have been made in Zagreb to establish mechanisms for cooperation among independent agencies. For example, the former Development Corporation for South Zagreb,
unlike most urban-development corporations in other areas,
was not given exclusive responsibility for developing its area,
but was charged with coordinating all the regular operating
agencies as they functioned in it. The annual site-preparation
plan, the Communal Utilities Fund, and the Institute of Communal Utilities attempt to bring many agencies into harmony
for specific purposes. This approach avoids some of the most
obvious problems arising from agency insulation and lack of
operating cooperation that are experienced in urban projects
in many areas--particularly in developing nations. Even
though implementation of the urban program in Zagreb tends
to fall behind its targets, the activities of various operating
agencies are phased in with each other and their agreement
to particular work programs is obtained. There are mechanisms in Zagreb for resolving interagency conflict or lack of
cooperation, which in other areas often delays projects even
after their financing has been authorized.

One aspect of functional decentralization that is of particular concern to city authorities is the fragmentation of urban public finance into various special funds and independent

budgets. A special fund has the advantage of making the activity financed more independent of the general government bureaucracy and so is particularly suited to the Yugoslav theory of self-government. Second, it renders financing arrangements both more flexible (such funds are not bound by traditionally rigid budgeting procedures of general government) and more stable (revenues tend to vary less than government revenues, which are subject to controversial allocation of shared resources among governments at different levels).

On the other hand, the complexity of local financing from rents, corporate user charges, social-insurance contributions, and earmarked taxes, all of which do not pass through the general government budgets, make it difficult to obtain a coherent picture of the financial situation of local administration as a whole and to conduct responsible and comprehensive fiscal policy. It weakens the city's control over urban services for which it has legal responsibility. Zagreb financial officials complain that the system presents some thorny problems of financial coordination, that individual institutions exercise fiscal decision-making on the basis of narrower criteria than the city would, that no one exercises effective control over their financial planning, and finally, that considerable duplication and wasted effort is entailed.

At the same time, it is argued that the financial autonomy of administrative institutions is a prerequisite of administrative and functional autonomy and, ultimately, of an open-market relationship among local public services. This attempt to approximate a market situation in urban-development and public-service activity is based on the hypothesis that in the long run it might be more conducive to efficiency than bureaucratic control. This is a unique experiment in urban administration. Its evaluation must await the passage of time, but it should be of major interest to scholars and practitioners in other nations of the world.

Processes of administrative reform in Zagreb have been remarkably elastic, in any case. During 1965 alone, following national economic liberalization, planning procedures were loosened up in Zagreb; several agencies were merged, creating, for example, the Zagreb Center for Economic Development and Institute of Communal Utilities; organization for housing investment and management was split into housing enterprises; school financing was for some time tied back into government budgets; some personnel decisions were delegated to employee councils within government departments; local budget units were shifted into finance departments, and direct employees of the city government were reduced by half.

In so far as popular participation is concerned, there are probably more people involved more frequently in official discussion on urban policies in Zagreb than in any other area examined in this series.

Citizens have been called upon to take part frequently in voters' meetings, assembly councils, house councils, school boards, neighborhood councils, and political organizations, as well as in the councils of the enterprises in which they work. Because of rotating membership in local assemblies, a large number of people are involved directly in local-government activities. In addition, consultation with various nongovernment organizations is built into many of the planning and decision-making procedures of local government. The degree of "direct democracy" has perhaps been developed to the point of diminishing returns, where citizens' available time for public activities is fully utilized and beyond which it is difficult to assemble a quorum.

In nations where a multiparty system is designed to channel citizen participation through formal political organizations, political parties are often not directly concerned with urban policy issues, even in local election campaigns. In most of our case areas, local party competition is cast for the most part in terms of national or ideological issues.

Moreover, at a time when the role of professional and technical administrators is growing in most urban areas in relation to that of elected representatives and politicians, Zagreb is attempting to reinstate the ascendancy of the representative assemblies. In Yugoslav theory, the technical services should operate with a minimum of nonprofessional interference, but professional administrators should not control social policies.

Organizing urban administration so as to maintain control by representative bodies over important policies, but to preserve the professional integrity of highly technical decisions is an extremely difficult task. For example, in Paris

local mayors complain that a larger and larger proportion of
decisions are made within the civil service and that the political responsibility of mayors and elected councils is withering.
On the other hand, in Calcutta the elected council interferes
directly in all minor appointments and minor expenditures by
the line departments. In Zagreb, there is no day-to-day
interference by the assembly organs, for department heads
have adequate management decision-making powers within
the scope of the approved budget and job plans and there is
no single or strong chief executive. The power of the assembly, on the other hand, is being enhanced by the super-
visory role of its executive councils, the limitation on the
term of appointment of top administrative officers, and the
involvement of public groups in the planning process. The
frequent turnover in local assembly members and prohibition
against election of local-government administrators has reduced the dominance of the bureaucracy in the assemblies.
Finally, the political organizations influence both personnel
and major management decisions. [3]

Taken altogether, functional decentralization, territorial
decentralization, and high citizen participation in Zagreb have
been accompanied by a slowing down of administrative procedures. But Zagreb is following these paths in reaction to
negative aspects of overcentralization and overconcentration
of bureaucratic power.

In any case, Zagreb is notable because its administrators
and policy-makers are consciously wrestling with the problems of organization in terms of both administrative efficiency
and political principles. The answers to many of the questions
raised are elusive. Would it be possible to achieve social
democracy at a lower administrative cost? Is the numerical
expression of popular participation a satisfactory index of real
participation? What loss of efficiency or administrative draw-
backs can actually be attributed to the establishment of urban
communes? Are there advantages in communal administration
being closer to the citizen that counterbalance the losses?
These are unanswered questions that have been posed in
similar terms in cities around the world.

In summary, Zagreb has several significant administrative advantages. It has an administrative and planning jurisdiction that encompasses the whole urban complex as well as land for future development, and has adequate power to provide coordination and metropolitan services. The Zagreb District is a regional as well as metropolitan jurisdiction and will thus be able in the future to integrate rural settlements with the city and undertake programs that might reduce the acceleration of migration into the urban center. There is high citizen participation in urban policy issues and safeguarded representative powers. Without the red tape of detailed supervision and central interference, intergovernmental relationships are relatively smooth and coordinated due to planning, legal regulation, general financial control, and unified political organization. The relationship between planning and budgeting is close. Personnel in the local civil service are of relatively high caliber. Land speculation and uncontrolled land development has been largely eliminated. There is an increasingly effective planning system for both short and long spans, and for physical, economic, and social development factors. And finally, important urban services are self-supporting.

Zagreb's administrative problems are related to four issues: streamlining the division of powers between communes and the city in order to eliminate duplication and put each operation at the level at which it can be most effectively provided; establishing effective coordinating devices for the proliferating special agencies and independent institutions; resolving conflicts and achieving consensus on major development issues in order to provide a policy foundation for long-range improvement programming within each major urban-service category; and finally, protecting the city's policy-development role.

## NOTES TO CHAPTER 6

1.    This plan was adopted in 1967 when the communes within the City of Zagreb were abrogated to create a single metropolitan-scale municipality, as is pointed out in the postscript to this book.

2.    This arrangement would approximate the Parisian intercommunal special districts for water, and other widely used special agencies, such as those for transit that are operating in Paris and proposed in Stockholm and used in several United States cities.

3.    Unlike most multiparty systems, the Yugoslav system is not beset with problems of partisanship entering into administrative decisions.  Therefore, Zagreb can probably operate more effectively with a close relationship between party and administration.  Much of the conflict and competition that is between parties in these other areas occurs in Yugoslavia within the League of Communists and the Socialist Alliance.

# POSTSCRIPT

A common difficulty in governmental studies is the constantly changing character of the subject matter. This is particularly true of urban areas in the mid-twentieth century, and fundamental changes have been occurring in Zagreb at a quicker pace than in most.

Since writing of this book was completed in late 1966, important modifications in the administrative organization of Zagreb, foreshadowed in the study's conclusions, have taken place. Urban Zagreb is now legally a single municipality.

In addition, the Republic of Croatia has abolished districts within its territory, with the result that the City of Zagreb--now encompassing the nine former urban communes-- is no longer a district authority over the adjoining rural communes.

The school funds have been replaced by "education associations," giving the school system greater financial and operational autonomy from general local government; and a more flexible system of bank investment in housing has been introduced. In elections for the Zagreb City Assembly held in April, 1967, 698 candidates contested 280 seats.

Finally, amendments to the federal constitution have changed the composition of the Federal Executive Council and of federal administration.

Governmental development in Zagreb is likely to continue to be dynamic in the near future. Work is currently under way to establish the new, geographically unified but functionally decentralized metropolitan government. An interesting topic for the student of administration is which institutions of local government have been more subject to change, and which more stable. This, however, would require another study.

July, 1967

## ABOUT THE AUTHORS

Eugen Pusić was born in Zagreb in 1916. Immediately after World War II, he was in charge of the Organization Bureau of the City of Zagreb and then of its Social Welfare Department. After several assignments in the administration of the republic, he became Professor of Public Administration at the University of Zagreb, where he is currently Dean of the Advanced School of Public Administration. He has served repeatedly as consultant to the Secretary-General of the United Nations, and is a fellow of the Institute of Social Studies in The Hague. His publications include books and monographs on general administration, local administration in Yugoslavia, and American government, as well as contributions to volumes published in The Netherlands and in Canada.

Annmarie Hauck Walsh is a member of the research staff of the Institute of Public Administration, New York, and director of its International Urban Studies Project. At the Institute, she has participated in a wide range of studies dealing with urban affairs, including urban transportation and outdoor recreation resources in American metropolitan areas. During three years of research in comparative urban administration, she has traveled in Europe and Africa and participated in several field studies.

The Institute of Public Administration, New York, is a private, nonprofit educational and research institution. It is the oldest professional center of its type in the United States, originally founded as the N. Y. Bureau of Municipal Research in 1906. Its work in recent years has been focused on research and technical assistance on government organization and policy problems and urban and human resource development.